Increasing Human Efficiency In Business

A Contribution To The Psychology Of Business

By
Walter Dill Scott

CHAPTER I

THE POSSIBILITY OF INCREASING HUMAN EFFICIENCY

THE modern business man is the true heir of the old magicians. Every thing he touches seems to increase ten or a hundredfold in value and usefulness. All the old methods, old tools, old instruments have yielded to his transforming spell or else been discarded for new and more effective substitutes. In a thousand industries the profits of to-day are wrung from the wastes or unconsidered trifles of yesterday.

The only factor which has withstood this wizard touch is man himself. Development of the instruments of production and distribution has been so great it can hardly be <p 1> <p 2> measured: the things themselves have been so changed that few features of their primitive models have been retained.

Our railroad trains, steamships, and printing presses preserve a likeness more apparent than actual. Our telephones, electric lights, gas engines, and steam turbines, our lofty office buildings and huge factories crowded with wonderful automatic machinery are creations of the generation of business men and scientists still in control of them.

By comparison the increase in human efficiency during this same period (except where the worker is the slave of the machine, compelled to keep pace with it or lose his place) has been insignificant.

Reasons for this disproportion are not lacking. The study of the physical antedates the study of the mental always. In the history of the individual as well as of nations, knowledge of the psychical has dragged far behind mastery of tangible objects. We come in contact with our physical environment and adjust ourselves to it long before we begin to <p 7> study the *acts by which we have been able to control objects around us.

It was inevitable, therefore, that attention should have been concentrated upon the material and mechanical side of production and distribution. Results there were so tangible, so easily figured. For example, if the speed of a drill or the strokes of a punch press were multiplied, the increase would be easily recognized. The whole country, too, was absorbed in invention, in the development of tools to accomplish what had always required hand labor. The effort was not so much to increase the efficiency of the individual worker— though many wise and far-sighted employers essayed studies and experiments with varying success—as to displace the human factor altogether.

As the functions and limitations of machinery have become clearer in recent years, business men have generally recognized the importance of the human factor in making and marketing products. Selecting and handling men is of much more significance to-day <p 4> than ever before in the history of the world —the more so as organizations have increased in size and scope and the individual employee is farther removed from the head and assigned greater responsibilities.

It is not a difficult task to build and equip a factory, to choose and stock a store. The problems of power and its transmission come nearer solution every day. Physics and chemistry have revealed the secrets of raw materials. For any given service, the manufacturer can determine the cheapest and most suitable metal, wood, or fabric which will satisfy his requirements, and the most economical method of treating it.

Of the elements involved in production or distribution, the human factor is to-day the most serious problem confronting the business man. The individual remains to be studied, trained, and developed—to be brought up to the standard of maximum results already reached by materials and processes.

Few employers can gather a force of effi- <p 5> cient workers and keep them at their best. Not only is it difficult to select the right men but it is even harder to secure top efficiency after they are hired. Touching this, there will be no dispute. Experts in shop management go even farther. F. W. Taylor, who has made the closest and most scientific study, perhaps, of actual and potential efficiency among workers, declares that:—

``A first-class man can, in most cases, do from two to four times as much as is done on the average.''

``This enormous difference,'' Mr. Taylor goes on to say, ``exists in all the trades and branches of labor investigated, from pick- and-shovel men all the way up the scale to machinists and other skilled workmen. The multiplied output was not the product of a spurt or a period of overexertion; it was simply what a good man could keep up for a long term of years without injury to his health, become happier, and thrive under.''

Ask the head of any important business what is the first qualification of a foreman <p 6> or manager, and he will tell you ``ability to handle men.''

Men who know how to get maximum results out of machines are common; the power to get the maximum of work out of subordinates or out of yourself is a much rarer possession.

Yet this power is not necessarily a sixth sense or a fixed attribute of personality. It is based on knowledge of the workings of the other man's mind, either intuitive or acquired. It is the purpose of this and succeeding chapters to consider some of the aspects of human nature that can be turned to advantage in the cultivation of individual efficiency and the elimination of lost motion and wasted effort.

In a thousand instances, in factory and market place, unrecognized use has been made of the principles of psychology by business men to influence other men and to attain their ends.

For the science of psychology is in respect to certain data merely common sense, the wisdom of experience, analyzed, formulated, and codified. <p 7> It has taken its place, alongside physics and chemistry, as the ally and employee of trade and industry.

The time has come when a man's knowledge of his business, if the larger success is to be won, must embrace an understanding of the laws which govern the thinking and acting of the men who make and sell his products as well as those others who buy and consume them.

The achievements of the human mind and the human body seem to many to be out of the range of possible improvement through application of any science which deals with these human activities. Muscular strength and mental efficiency seem to be fixed quantities not subject to increase or improvement.

The contention here supported, however, is that human efficiency is a variable quantity which increases and decreases according to law. By the application of known physical laws the telephone and the telegraph have supplanted the messenger boy. By the laws of psychology applied to business equally astounding improvements are being and will be secured. <p 8>

Employers sometimes find that their men are not working well, that they loaf and kill time on every possible occasion. The men are not trying and are indifferent to results. Under such circumstances a new foreman, the dismissal of the poorer workmen, modification of the wage scale or method of payment, or some other device may correct the evil and induce the men to exert themselves.

Again, the men are working industriously and may feel that an increase in output would be injurious to health or even impossible. They think they are doing their best; while the employer himself may feel that he is achieving but little, although he assumes that he is doing as much as it is wise to attempt. For instance, Mr. Taylor, in his studies, found that both employers and men had only a vague conception of what constituted a full day's work for a first-class man. The good workmen knew they could do more than the average; but refused to believe when, after close observation and careful timing of the ele- <p 9> ments of each operation, they were shown that they could accomplish twice or three times as much as their customary tasks.

Actual instances prove that great increase of work and results can be secured by outside stimulus and by conscious effort.

If there is one place where the limit of exertion can be counted upon, it is in an inter- collegiate athletic contest. While taking part in football games, I frequently observed that my team would be able to push the opposing team halfway across the field. Then the tables would be turned and my team would give ground. At one moment one team would seem to possess much superior physical strength to the other; the next moment the equilibrium would be changed apparently without cause. Often, however, the weaker team would rally in response to the captain's coaching. On the field a player frequently finds himself unable to exert himself. His greatest effort is necessary to force himself to work. In such a mental condition a vigorous and enthusiastic appeal from the coach may <p 10> supply the needed stimulus and stir him to sudden display of all his strength.

I recently conducted a series of experiments on college athletes to determine whether coaching could actually increase a man's strength when he was already trying his ``best,'' and whether he could continue to work after he was ``completely exhausted.'' I put each man at work on machines which allowed him to exert himself to his utmost and measured his accomplishment. While he was thus employed, the coach began urging him to increase his exertion. Ordinarily the increase was marked—sometimes as much as fifty per cent.

Again, when the man had exhausted himself without coaching, the extra demand would be made on him; usually he was able to continue, even though without the coaching he had been unable to do any more. There was, of course, a point of exhaustion at which the coaching ceased to be effective.

The tests proved conclusively that when a man is doing what he believes to be his best, he is still <p 11> able to do better; when he is completely exhausted, he is, under proper stimulus, able to continue.

Before a horse is started in a race it is vigorously exercised, ``warmed up." To the uninitiated this process seems so strenuous as to defeat its purpose by wearing out the strength of the horse. Every horseman knows, however, that the animal cannot attain top speed till after it has undergone this severe discipline.

In training for a contest an athlete usually takes long runs. Soon after the start he feels weary and exhausted, but, by disregarding this feeling and continuing to run, a sudden change comes over him commonly known as ``getting his second wind."

Thus the runner feels wave upon wave of exhaustion followed by waves of invigoration. Had he stopped when he first began to tire, he never would have known of his wonderful reserve fund of strength which can be drawn upon only by passing through the feeling of exhaustion. He seems to be able to tap deeper and deeper reservoirs of strength. <p 12>

Many men have never discovered their reserve stores of strength because they have formed the fixed habit of quitting at the first access of weariness.

Thus they never become conscious of the wonderful resources which might be used if they were willing to disregard the trifling wave of weariness.

Our best energies are not on the surface and are not available without great exertion. We have to warm up and get our second wind before we are capable of our best physical or mental accomplishments. All our muscular and psychical processes are dependent upon the activity of the nervous system. This activity seems to be at its best only after repeated and vigorous stimulation and after it has reached down to profound and widely distributed centers.

Most of us never know of our possible achievements because we have never warmed up and got our second wind in our business or professional affairs.

When an individual succeeds in tapping his <p 13> reserve energies, others marvel at the tremendous tasks he accomplishes. They judge in terms of superficial energy, and for such the results would, of course, be impossible, even though many of the admiring spectators could actually equal or excel the deed.

Consider for a moment the work achieved by Mr. Edward Payson Weston who recently walked the entire distance from New York to San Francisco without halt or rest in one hundred and four days. Throughout the entire journey Mr. Weston covered about fifty miles daily, once attaining the remarkable distance of eighty-seven miles in twenty-four hours. Though Mr. Weston is seventy years of age, at the close of the walk he seemed to be relatively free from exhaustion and undaunted in spirit.

The work accomplished by such men as Gladstone and Roosevelt is incomprehensible to most of us who have never undertaken more than puny tasks. These men retain their strength and in no way seem to be undermining their health by the accomplishment of their <p 14> Herculean labors. Body and mind seem to respond to the demands made upon them. Their periods of sleep and their vacations seem to be no more than the hours and days of rest required by those of us who accomplish infinitely less.

No need, however, to go beyond the field of business or industry to find men whose super-energy has carried them to epochial discoveries or feats of organization. The invention of the incandescent lamp by Edison is said to have been accomplished, for instance, only after forty-eight hours' continuous concentration on the final problem of finding the right carbon filament and determining the proper degree of vacuum in the inclosing bulb. Months of experiment and research had gone before; eighteen hours a day in the laboratory had been no uncommon thing for the inventor and his assistants, but in the last strenuous grapple with success his own physical and mental powers were alone equal to the strain. Not once during the two days and nights did he rest or sleep or take his attention <p 15> from the successive tests which led up to the assembling of the lamp which lights the world's work and play.

The steel blade that is used seems to last as long as the one which is allowed to lie idle. The wearing out in the one case does not seem to be more destructive than the rusting out in the other.

We have a choice between wearing out and rusting out. Most of us unwittingly have chosen the rusting process.

This, indeed, may be said to be Edison's regular method of work, as it is the method of many other men who have accomplished great things in science and industry. Both mind and body have been trained and accustomed to exertions which seem quite impossible to ordinary individuals.

Many persons find that increased intellectual activity results in less fatigue and greater achievements. As a student I did my best work and enjoyed it most the year I carried the greatest number of courses and assumed the most outside duties. In my <p 16> capacity as adviser to college students I find many who are able to accomplish thirty per cent more work than is expected of college students but fail to do equally well the regular amount. There are others who can carry the regular amount but not more without injury to their health.

College grades afford a means of recording intellectual efficiency directed toward particular problems. With no apparent change in bodily conditions the same student frequently increases his efficiency a hundred per cent. The increase seldom has an injurious effect on health, but is merely evidence of the fact that he has suddenly wakened up and is applying energies which before were undiscovered. A slow walk for a single mile leaves many persons ``dragged out" and exhausted, but a brisk walk of the same or a greater distance results in invigoration and recuperation. Likewise the droning over an intellectual task results in exhaustion, while vigorous treatment whets the appetite for additional problems.

This swift, decisive attack on problems was <p 17> the method of Edward H. Harriman, who crowded into ten years the railroad achievements of an extraordinary lifetime. Decisions involving expenditure of many millions of dollars were arrived at so quickly as to seem off-hand, even reckless. In reality, they were the products of brief periods of intense application in which he reviewed all the conditions and elements involved, and forged his conclusion, as it were, at white heat. Back of each decision was exact and thorough knowledge of the physical and traffic conditions of each of his railroads. In the case of the Union Pacific, at least, he gained this mastery by patient, intensive study of each grade and curve and freight-producing town on its 1800 miles of track.

The inhabitant of the torrid zone upon moving to a northern climate is severely affected by the chill of the atmosphere. The discomfort may last for days or months, but he becomes acclimated and is able to withstand the cold without serious discomfort. Likewise the inhabitant of a cool climate feels exhausted <p 18> by the heat of the torrid zone. In some cases he is unable to accustom himself to the change, but in many instances the acclimatization follows rapidly and leaves the individual well fortified against the dangers of excessive heat.

Persons who have accustomed themselves to stimulants of any sort are completely depleted if they are unable to get the special form to which they have been accustomed. This holds true for tobacco, morphine, coffee, and many other forms of stimulants actually indulged in by many persons. If they are able to resist the temptation and deny themselves the stimulant, the period of exhaustion soon disappears and the subject may even lose all craving for that which formerly seemed essential to his very existence.

The quantity which we eat is partly a matter of habit. There is doubtless a minimum of nourishment which is absolutely necessary for health and strength. On the other hand there is doubtless a maximum limit which cannot be passed without serious injury. Our bodies seem to demand the amount of <p 19> food to which we have accustomed them. If we should increase the amount ten or twenty per cent, we might, for a while, feel some discomfort from it, but soon our system would begin to demand the greater quantity and we could not again return to the lighter diet without a period of discomfort. Likewise the amount of food which most of us consume could be reduced materially with no permanent injury or reduction of energy or danger to health. Following the reduction would be a period of discomfort and probable reduction of weight. This period would last for but a relatively short time, after which we would again strike a physiological equilibrium such that an increase of food would not be craved nor be of any benefit.

Any great increase in the amount of physical or mental work results in a feeling of weariness which is usually sufficient to cause us to return to our habitual amount of expenditure of energy. Our system is, however, wonderful in its capacity to adjust itself to changed demands which come upon it, whether these <p 20> demands be in the nature of changes in temperature, in stimulants, in nourishment, or in the expenditure of physical or mental energy.

There is, of course, a limit to possible human achievements. There are resources which may not be exhausted without serious injury to health. Those who accomplish most, however, compare favorably with others in length of days and retention of health.

While overwork has its place among the things which reduce energy and shorten life, it is my opinion that overwork is not so dangerous or so common as is ordinarily supposed.

In not a few industries, the dominant house or firm has for its head a man past seventy who still keeps a firm and vigorous grip on the business: men like Richard T. Crane of Chicago, E. C. Simmons of St. Louis, and James J. Hill, whose careers are records of intense industry and absorbed devotion to the work in hand.

Many persons confuse overwork with what is really underwork accompanied with worry or unhygienic practices. <p 21>

A recent writer on sociology calls attention to the fact that nervous prostrations and general breakdowns are most common among those members of society who achieve the least and who may be regarded as parasites. Exercise both of brain and of muscle is necessary for growth and for health.

Those nations which expend the most energy are probably the ones among whom longevity is greatest and the mortality rate the lowest. In the city of Chicago there are many conditions adverse to health of body and mind, yet the city is famous for its relatively low mortality as a parallel fact. It is also affirmed that the average Chicago man works longer hours and actually accomplishes more than the average man elsewhere. This excess in the expenditure of energy—in so far as it is wisely spent—may be one of the reasons for the excellent health record of the city.

In every walk of life we see that the race is not to the swift nor the battle to the strong. We all know men clearly of secondary ability who nevertheless occupy high positions in <p 22> business and state. We are acquainted also with men of excellent native endowment who still have never risen above the ranks of mediocrity.

Human efficiency is not measured in terms of muscular energy nor of intellectual grasp. It is dependent upon many factors other than native strength of mind and body.

The attitude which one takes toward life in general and toward his calling in particular is of more importance than native ability. The man with concentration, or the power of continued enthusiastic application, will surpass a brilliant competitor if this latter is careless and indifferent towards his work. Many who have accomplished great things in business, in the professions, and in science have been men of moderate ability. For testimony of this fact take this striking quotation from Charles Darwin.

``I have no great quickness of apprehension or wit, which is so remarkable in some clever men," he writes. ``I am a poor critic. . . . My power to follow a long and purely abstract <p 23> train of thought is very limited; and therefore I never could have succeeded with metaphysics or mathematics. My memory is extensive, yet hazy; it suffices to make me cautious by vaguely telling me that I have observed or read something opposed to the conclusion which I am drawing, or on the other hand in favor of it. So poor in one sense is my memory, that I have never been able to remember for more than a few days a single date or a line of poetry. I have a fair share of invention, and of common sense or judgment, such as every fairly successful lawyer or doctor must have, but not, I believe, in any higher degree."

This is presumably an honest statement of fact, and in addition it should be remembered that Darwin was always physically weak, that for forty years he was practically an invalid and able to work for only about three hours a day. In these few hours he was able to accomplish more, however, than other men of apparently superior ability who were able to work long hours daily for many <p 24> years. Darwin made the most of his ability and increased his efficiency to its maximum.

For a parallel in business, Cyrus H. McCormick might be named. The inventor of the reaper and builder of the first American business which covered the world was not a man of extraordinary intellect, wit, or judgment. He had, however, the will and power to focus his attention on a single question until the answer was evolved. Again and again, his biographers tell us, he pursued problems which eluded him far into the night and he was frequently found asleep at his desk the morning following. When roused, instead of seeking rest, he addressed his task again and usually overcame his obstacle before leaving it.

All these considerations point to one conclusion. It is quite certain, then, that most of us are whiling away our days and occupying positions far below our possibilities. A corollary to this statement is Mr. Taylor's conclusion that ``few of our best-organized industries have attained the maximum output of first-class men." <p 25>

Not to give too wide application to his discovery that the average day's work is only half or less than half what a first-class man can do, it is more than probable that the average man could, with no injury to his health, increase his efficiency fifty per cent.

We are making use of only part of our existing mental and physical powers and are not taxing them beyond their strength. Increased accomplishments, and heightened efficiency would cultivate and develop them, would waken the latent powers and tap hidden stores of energy within us, would widen the fields in which we labor and would open up to us new and wider horizons of honorable and profitable activity.

In succeeding chapters will be described specific methods, many of which are employed by individual firms, but which could be utilized by other business men, to insure their own efficiency and that of their employees. The experiences of many successful houses will be linked to the laws of psychology to point the way that will bring about greater results from men.

CHAPTER II

IMITATION

AS A MEANS OF INCREASING HUMAN EFFICIENCY

TWENTY years ago the head of an industry now in the million-a-month class sat listening to his ``star'' salesman. The latter, in the first enthusiasm of discovery and creation, was telling how he had developed the company's haphazard selling talk and had taken order after order with a standard approach, demonstration, and summary of closing arguments. To prove the effectiveness of ``the one best way,'' he challenged his employer to act as a customer, staged the little drama he had arranged, secured admissions of savings his machine would make, ultimately cornered the other, and sold him.

``That's great," the owner declared the in- <p 26> <p 27> stant he had surrendered to the salesman's logic. ``If we can get all our agents to learn and use this new method of yours, we'll double our business in three years."

Then followed discussion of the means by which the knowledge could be spread.

``I've got it," the manager announced at last. ``I'll telegraph five or six men to come in"—he named the agents within a night's ride of the factory—``and you can show them how you sold fifteen machines last week.

``We could take down your talk in shorthand and send it to them, but that wouldn't do the business. I want them to watch you sell, to study how you make your points, how you introduce yourself, how you get your man's attention, how you bring out his objections and meet them, how you lead up to the signing minute, and show him where to sign. *What you say is about half the trick: *how you say it is the convincing part—the thing the slowest man in the force by watching you can learn more quickly than the smartest could work out at home." <p 28>

The result of that conference was one of the earliest organized training schools for salesmen in the country. It was an unconscious, but none the less certain, utilization of the instinct of *imitation for increasing the efficiency in employees. Since then, business has borrowed many well-recognized principles from psychology and pedagogy and adapted them to the same end.

Many important houses have grafted the school upon their organizations and *teach not only raw and untrained employees, but provide instruction calculated to make workmen and clerks masters of their jobs and also to fit them for advancement to higher and more productive planes. Teaching is by example rather than by precept, just as it was in the old apprentice system.

The newer method uses even more than the older a perfect example of the process and the product for the learner's imitation and makes them the basis of the instruction.

No man was made to live alone. For an individual, existence entirely independent of <p 29> other members of the race is the conception of a dreamer; apart from others one would fail to become *human. Modern psychology has abandoned the individualistic and adopted the social point of view. We no longer think of *imitation as a characteristic only of animals, children, and weak-minded folk.

We have come to see that imitation is the greatest factor in the education of the young and a continuous process with all of us. The part of wisdom, then, is to utilize this power from which we cannot escape, by setting up a perfect copy for imitation.

The child brought up by a Chinaman imitates the sounds he hears, hence speaks Chinese; brought up in an American home, English is his speech—ungrammatical or correct according to the usage of his companions. If one boy in a group walks on stilts or plays marbles, the others follow his example. If a social leader rides in an automobile, wears a Panama hat, or plays golf, all the members of this circle are restless till they have the same experience. The same <p 30> phenomenon is seen in the professions and in business. If one bank decides to erect a building for its own use, other banks in the city begin to consult architects. If one manufacturer or distributor in a given field adopts a new policy in manufacturing or in extending his trade zone, his rivals immediately consider plans of a similar sort. Partly, of course, this act is defensive. In the main, however, imitation and emulation are at the bottom of the move.

For the sake of clearness, in studying acts of imitation we separate them into two classes—*voluntary imitation (also called conscious imitation) and *instinctive imitation (also known as *suggestive imitation).

A peculiar signature may strike my fancy so that consciously and deliberately I may try to imitate it. This is a clear case of voluntary imitation. Threading crowded city streets, I see a man crossing at a particular point and voluntarily follow in his path. In learning a new skating figure I watch an expert attentively and try to repeat his perform- <p 31> ance. In writing letters or advertisements or magazine articles, I analyze the work of other men and consciously imitate what seems best. Or I observe a fellow-laborer working faster than I, and forthwith try to catch and hold his pace.

The contagion of yawning, on the other hand, is instinctive imitation. Also when in a crowd during the homeward evening rush, we instinctively quicken our pace though there may be no reason for hurry.

For precisely similar reasons, a ``loafer" or a careless or inefficient workman will lower the efficiency or slow up the production of the men about him, no matter how earnest or industrious their natural habits. Night work by clerks, also, is taken by some office managers to indicate a slump in industry during the day. To correct this the individuals who are drags on the organization are discovered, and either are revitalized or discharged.

I have seen more than one machine shop where production could have been materially raised <p 32> by the simple expedient of weeding out the workmen who were satisfied with a mere living wage earned by piecework, *thereby setting a dilatory example to the rest; and replacing them with fresh men ambitious to earn all they could, who would have been imitated by the others.*

In these instances it is assumed that the imitation is not voluntary, but that we unconsciously imitate whatever actions happen to catch our attention. For the negative action, the ``slowing down" process, we have the greater affinity simply because labor or exertion is naturally distasteful. One such influence or example, therefore, may sway us more than a dozen positive impulses towards industry.

Imitation thus broadly considered is seen to be of the utmost importance in every walk of life. The greatest and most original genius is in the main a creature of imitation. By imitation he reaches the level of knowledge and skill attained by others; and upon this foundation builds his structure of original and creative thought, experiment, and achieve- <p 33> ment. Furthermore he does not imitate at random; but concentrates his activity on those things and persons in the line of his pursuits.

Among my associates are both industrious and shiftless individuals. I instinctively imitate the actions of all those with whom I come in contact; but if I am sufficiently ambitious, I will consciously imitate the acts of the industrious. This patterning after energetic models will render me more active and efficient than would have been possible for me without such examples.

Imitation, accordingly, is an imperative factor both in self-development and in the control of groups of individuals. Knowing that I instinctively imitate all sorts of acts, I must take care that only the right sort shall catch my attention.

And since imitation is a most effective aid in development, I must provide myself with the best models. To reduce my tendency to idleness or procrastination I must avoid the companionship of the shiftless. To acquire <p 34> ease and accuracy in the use of French, I must consort with masters of that tongue.

In handling others, the same rule holds.

To profit from the instinctive imitation of my men, I must control their environment in shop or office and make sure that examples of energy and efficiency are numerous enough to catch their attention and establish, as it were, an atmosphere of industry in the place.

There are instances in which it would be to the mutual interest of employer and employee to increase the speed of work, but conditions may limit or forbid the use of pacemakers. In construction work and in some of the industries where there are minute subdivision of operations and continuity of processes this method of increasing efficiency is very commonly applied. In many factories, however, such an effort to ``speed up" production might stir resentment, even among the pieceworkers, and have an effect exactly opposite to that desired. The alternative, of course, is for the employer to secure unconscious pacemakers by providing incentives <p 35> for the naturally ambitious men in the way of a premium or bonus system or other reward for unusual efficiency.

To take advantage of their conscious or voluntary imitation, workpeople must be provided with examples which appeal to them as admirable and inspire the wish to emulate them. A common application of this principle is seen in the choice of department heads, foremen, and other bosses. Invariably these win promotion by industry, skill, and efficiency greater than that displayed by their fellows, or by all-round mastery of their trades which enable them to show their less efficient mates how any and all operations should be conducted.

This focusing of attention upon individuals worthy of imitation has been carried much farther by various companies. Through their ``house organs"—weekly or monthly papers published primarily for circulation within the organization—they make record of every incident reflecting unusual skill, initiative, or personal power in an individual member of the organization. <p 36>

A big order closed, a difficult contract secured, a complex or delicate operation performed in less than the usual time, a new personal record in production, the invention of an unproved method or machine—whatever the achievement, it is described and glorified, its author praised and held up for emulation. This, indeed, is one of the methods by which the larger sales organizations have obtained remarkable results.

Graphically told, the story of an important sale with the salesman's picture alongside makes double use of the instinct of imitation. It suggests forcibly that every man in the field can duplicate the achievement and tells how he can do it.

Frequently, examples of initiative and efficiency are borrowed from outside organizations. ``Carrying a message to Garcia" has long been a business synonym for immediate and effective execution of orders. One big company, employing thousands of mechanics and developing all its executives and skilled experts from boys and men within the or- <p 37> ganization, has printed in its house organ studies of all the great American and English inventors from Stephenson and Fulton to Edison and Westinghouse. These histories emphasize the facts that these men were self-taught and bench-trained, and that their achievements can be imitated by every intelligent mechanic in the organization.

In teaching and learning by imitation certain modifying facts are to be kept constantly in mind. We tend to imitate everything which catches our attention, but certain things appeal more powerfully than others.

The acts of those whom I admire are particularly contagious, but I remain indifferent to the acts of those who are uninteresting. Acts showing a skill to which I aspire are immediately imitated, while acts representing stages of development from which I have escaped are less likely to be imitated. We imitate the acts of hearty, jovial individuals more than the acts of others. This point cannot be pressed too far since a surly and selfish individual often seems to corrupt a whole <p 38> group. Also it is not always the acts which I admire that are imitated. If I am frequently with a lame person, I am in danger of acquiring a limp; one who stutters is clearly injurious to my freedom of speech; round-shouldered friends may at first cause me to straighten up, but soon I am in danger of a droop.

That imitation is merely something to be avoided by teachers, employers, and foremen is an idea soon banished when the importance and complexity of the process is comprehended. In teaching we find precept inferior to example wherever the latter is possible. Particularly in teaching all sorts of acts of skill the imitation of perfect models is the first resort. In business, however, insufficient consideration has been given to the possibilities of imitation in increasing human efficiency.

In the preparation of this article representative business men who had been especially successful in dealing with employees were asked the following questions:— <p 39>

In increasing the efficiency of your employees do you utilize imitation by

(1) placing efficient workmen where they may be imitated by the less efficient?

(2) having the men visit highly efficient establishments?

(3) bringing to the attention of your men the lives of successful men and the work of successful houses?

(4) bringing frequently to the attention of the men model methods of work?

(5) Have you observed any pronounced instance of increase or decrease in the work of a department due to imitation?

The men interviewed took a decided interest in the subject, and their answers contained much of general value. Some admitted that they had never made any conscious effort to utilize imitation as implied in the first four questions. Many others had made particular use of one or more of the methods. A few of the firms interviewed had employed all four methods with entire satisfaction. <p 40>

The following is a fair representative of the answers. It is the response of a very successful general manager of a railroad:—

``I beg to give you below the answer to the questions which you have asked:—

``1. The superintendent and foremen in our shops are the most efficient we can find. They are imitated, and thus influence the less efficient.

``2. We have the heads of our departments visit other shops to see how they are progressing in the same line. If they notice anything that is better than what we have as to the output of work, we imitate it by following their methods.

``3. We have not made a practice of bringing to the attention of our employees the lives of successful men or the work of successful houses.

``4. We keep standard models of the different kinds of work in plain view of the men. If there is any doubt in their minds, they can study these models.

``5. We have observed a pronounced in- <p 41> crease in the work of our shops, due to imitation, since in lining up our organization we put the most competent men we have at the head. Their influence over the men in their charge increases the work, as there is no question that a good leader is imitated by the men, and the company is benefited by this imitation."

Judged by the results of the investigation the most common use of imitation is in the training or ``breaking in" of new employees. The accepted plan is to pick out the most expert and intelligent workman available and put the new man in his charge.

By observing the veteran and imitating his actions, working gradually from the simpler operations to the more complex, the beginner is able to master technic and methods in the shortest possible time. The psychological moment for such instruction, of course, is the first day or the first week. New men learn much more readily than those who have become habituated to certain methods or tasks; not having had time or opportunity to experi- <p 42> ment and learn wrong methods, they have nothing to unlearn in acquiring the right. They fall into line at once and adopt the stride and the manner of work approved by the house.

This is the specific process by which the most advanced industrial organizations develop machine hands and initiate skilled mechanics into house methods and requirements. It has been largely used by public service corporations—street-car motormen and conductors, for instance, learning their duties almost entirely by observation of experienced men either in formal schools or on cars in actual operation. Many large commercial houses give new employees regular courses in company methods before intrusting work to them; the instructor is some highly efficient specialist, who shows the beginner *how* to get output and quality with the least expenditure of time and energy. The same method has been adapted by leading manufacturers of machines, who call their mechanics or assemblers together at intervals and have the most <p 43> expert among them show how they conduct operations in which they have attained special skill.

In the training of salesmen imitation has received its widest application in teaching new men the elements of salesmanship; in showing them how to make the individual sale; in giving old men the best and newest methods— all by imitation.

Not only is the recruit to the selling ranks in formal schools given repeated examples of the most effective ways to approach customers, to demonstrate the house goods and secure the order; but the more progressive companies, after this preliminary instruction, assign him to a training ground where he accompanies one of the company's best salesmen and merely observes how actual sales are made. Then the new man is sent out alone; usually he fails to secure as large an order as the house wants. Again the star salesman takes him in hand, analyzes the student's approach and demonstration, points out their weaknesses and, going back with the new man, <p 44> makes the right kind of approach and secures a satisfactory order. For the beginner this is the most vivid lesson in salesmanship; he cannot but model his next selling effort on the lines proved so effective.

The use of imitation, however, is carried further. In the monthly or semiannual district conventions of salesmen which most big organizations call, the newest and most effective selling methods are staged for the instruction both of new men and veterans. The district leader in sales, for example, or the man who has closed an order by a new or unusual argument is pitted against a salesman equally able, and the whole force sees how the successful man secured his results.

Educational trips to other factories were employed by several firms to stimulate mental alertness and the instinct of imitation in their men. These trips usually supplemented some sort of suggestion system for encouraging employees to submit to the management ideas for improving methods, machines, or products.

Cash payments were made for each suggestion <p 45> adopted, quarterly prizes of ten to fifty dollars were awarded for the most valuable suggestions; and finally a dozen or a score of the men submitting the best ideas were sent on a week's tour of observation to other industrial centers and notable plants. In some instances the expense incurred was considerable, but the companies considered the money well spent. Not only were the men making helpful suggestions the very ones who would observe most wisely and profit most extensively from such educational trips, but they would bring back to their everyday tasks a new perspective, see them from a new angle, and frequently offer new suggestions which would more than save or earn the vacation cost.

Business managers, it was made plain, are coming more and more to depend upon imitation as one of the great forces in securing a maximum of efficiency without risking the rupture or rebellion which might follow if the same efficiency were sought by force or by any method of conscious compulsion. Tactfully suggested, the examples for imitation will <p 46> lead men where no amount of argument or reasonable compensation will drive them. I am therefore led to suggest the following uses of imitation for increasing the efficiency of the working force.

In breaking in new recruits they should be set to imitate expert workmen in all the details possible.

Gang foremen and superintendents should always be capable of ``showing how" for the sake of the men under them.

The better workmen should, where possible, be located so that they will be observed by the other employees.

Inefficient help should be avoided since the example of the less efficient should become the model for the larger group.

Educational trips or tours of inspection should be regularly encouraged for both workmen and superintendents.

The deeds of successful houses should be brought to the attention of employees.

Where conditions admit, pacemakers should be retained in various groups to key up the other men. <p 47>

Favorable conditions should be provided for conscious and instinctive imitation for all the members of the plant.

Persons who are sociable and much liked are imitated more than others, and if efficient, are particularly valuable; but if inefficient, are especially detrimental to others.

At the formal and informal meetings of the men of a house or a department, demonstrations of how to do certain definite things are very interesting and helpful to all concerned. Demonstrations should be more common.

CHAPTER III

COMPETITION

AS A MEANS OF INCREASING HUMAN EFFICIENCY

THIRTY years ago American steel makers were astonishing the world with new production records. What English ironmasters, intrenched in their supremacy for centuries, had regarded as a standard week's output for Bessemer converters, their young rivals in mills about the Great Lakes were doubling, trebling, and even further increasing. Hardly a month passed without a new high mark and a shift in possession of the leadership.

To this remarkable increase in efficiency William R. Jones—``Captain Bill" Jones as he was familiarly known—contributed more than any other operating man. He was a genius among executives as well as an inventor <p 48> <p 49> of resource and initiative—a natural leader and handler of men. When he was asked by the British Iron and Steel Institute in 1881, to explain the reasons for the amazing development in the United States, he attributed it to organization spirit of the workmen and the rivalry among the various mills.

``So long as the record made by a mill stands first," he wrote, ``its workmen are content to labor at a moderate rate. But let it be known that some other establishment has beaten that record and there is no content until the rival's record is eclipsed."

It was on this idea of competition for efficiency—of production as a game and achievement as a goal—that the wonderful growth of the steel industry was based.

On the intensive development of this idea by Andrew Carnegie, within his expanding organization, hinged the tremendous progress and profits of the Carnegie Company. ``The little boss" matched furnace against furnace, mill against mill, superintendent against superintendent. He scanned his weekly and <p 50> monthly reports not merely for records of output, but for comparative consumption of ore, fuel, and other supplies, for time and labor costs in proportion to product.

If a superintendent, foreman, or gang failed to respond to this urging, failed to get into the race for the famous broom which crowned the stack of the champion Carnegie mill or furnace, the parallel showing of the other mills became a club to drive the laggards into line. So intense was the competition, so sharp the verbal goads applied that Jones, after resigning in indignation, parodied in sarcastic notes in this manner the Carnegie fashion of bringing executives to task: ``Puppy dog number three, you have been beaten by puppy dog number two on fuel. Puppy dog number two, you are higher on labor than puppy dog number one."

How effective was this system of pitting man against man, plant against plant, was shown by the dominant position of the Carnegie Company in the trade when the Steel Corporation was launched and by the stag- <p 51> gering value put upon its business. Indirect testimony of the same fact was given another time by Jones when he refused thousands of dollars in yearly royalties for the use of his inventions by outside companies, this though the men who sought them were personal friends and his contract with the Carnegie Company allowed such licenses. His excuse was eloquent of the power residing in the Carnegie contest for efficiency and results: leadership for his charge, the Edgar Thompson works, in output and costs, meant more to him than money and a chance to help his friends.

The Carnegie system was one of the most comprehensive applications in business of man's instinct of competition to the work of increasing individual and organization efficiency.

In the handling of executives it was carried to such extremes as few great managers would approve to-day. Undeniably, however, the contest idea was an important influence in the building up of a vast business in relatively brief time, while the influence on the pace of the whole industry gave the United States its <p 52> present supremacy in steel and iron. It survives in the parallel comparisons of records with which the Steel Corporation measures the efficiency of its units of production and keeps its mill superintendents to the mark. It is utilized, in some degree and in varying departments, by hundreds of successful houses.

Let us analyze the facts, the habits of thought, the emotions behind competition and determine where and how it may be applied to the task of increasing our own and our employees' efficiency.

The experienced horseman knows that a horse is unable to attain his greatest speed apart from a pacemaker. The horse needs the stimulus of an equal to get under way quickly, to strike his fastest gait and to keep it up. In this particular an athlete in sprinting is like the horse. He is unable by sheer force of will to run a hundred yards in ten seconds. To achieve it he needs a competitor who will push him to his utmost effort.

The struggle for existence, one of the main factors in the evolution of man, has raged most <p 53> fiercely among equals; without it, development scarcely would have been possible.

So fundamental has been this struggle that the necessity for it has become firmly established within us. We require it to stimulate us to attain our highest ends.

As is made evident by a consideration of imitation we are eminently social creatures. We imitate the acts of those about us. Imitation is, however, only the first stage of our social relationship. We first imitate and then compete. I purchase an automobile in imitation of the acts of my friends, but I compete with them by securing a more powerful or swifter car. By erecting a new building because some other banker has done so, the second individual does more than imitate. He competes with the first by planning to erect a more magnificent structure and on a more commanding site. Or a great retail store, announcing a ``February sale" of ``white goods" or furniture, invariably tries to surpass the bargains offered by rival establishments. <p 54>

We do indeed imitate and compete with all our associates, but those whom we recognize as our peers are the ones who stimulate us more to the instinctive acts of imitation and competition.

Our actual equals stimulate us less than those whom we recognize as the peers of our ideal selves—of ourselves as we strive and intend to become. The man on the ladder just above me stirs me irresistibly.

The effect of one individual upon others, then, is not confined to imitation. There is a constant tendency to vary from and to excel the model. My devotion to golf is mainly due to he example of some of my friends. My ambition is to outplay these same friends. Imitation and competition, apparently antagonistic, are in reality the two expressions for our social relationships. We first imitate and then attempt to differentiate ourselves from our companions.

The manufacturer or merchant imitates his competitor, but tries also to surpass him. Indeed it is a truism that competition is the <p 55> life of trade. In the shop and in the office, on the road and behind the counter, in all buying and selling, competition is essential to the greatest success. Competition, the desire to excel, is universal and instinctive. It gives a zest to our work that would otherwise be lacking. In every sphere of human activity competition seems essential for securing the best results.

We assume ordinarily that competition exists only between individuals. As a matter of fact, a slight degree of competition may be aroused between a man's present efforts and his previous records.

While not so tense or so compelling as is competition between individuals, it has the advantage of avoiding the creation of jealousies. In all the more exciting and stimulating games, rivalry between individuals is a prominent feature. In golf the game is frequently played without this factor, the only competition being with previous records or with the mythical Bogy.

Such competition adds considerable zest <p 56> to the game, and the same principle is applicable to business. The most compelling rivalry is between peers; without this, however, it is possible to pit the possibilities of the present month against the achievements of the previous four weeks or the past year or even against a hypothetical individual ``bogy.'' This bogy may be fixed by the executive, and the man induced to compete with it. Thus the dangers of competition may be minimized and the advantages of the human instinctive desire for competition be gained.

In the average well-organized business the carrying out of such a plan would not be difficult. Studying the previous records of his men, a manager or foreman could determine what each individual bogy should be. The employee should know just what the *record is that he is competing with, and that his success or failure would be recorded to his credit or otherwise. Above all, the bogy must be fair and within the power of the man to accomplish.

Competition need not be confined to individuals. <p 57> *Frequently one city finds a stimulus in competing with another. Nations compete with one another. In any organization one section may compete with another.*

In an army there may be competition between regiments. Within the regiment there may be the keenest rivalry between the different companies. We are such social creatures that we easily identify ourselves with our block, our street, our town, our social set, our party, our firm, or our department in the firm. Like teams in any game or sport, these groups may be rendered self-conscious and thus made units for competition.

It is possible to create such units for competition in business organizations. In some instances individual employees of one firm are pitted against those of a competing firm, the contest proving stimulating to the men in both. In other instances the competition is restricted to the house, and similar departments or sections are the units.

The closer the parallel between the units and their activities, as in the Carnegie blast <p 58> furnaces and steel mills, the more interesting and effective the competition becomes.

This principle has received widest recognition and achieved greatest success in the sales department. Here individuals are on a footing of approximate equality or may be given equality by a system of handicaps based on conditions in their territories. Success has also attended the pitting of selling districts against each other. These larger competing units work against bogies of the same character as do the individual ones. The whole house may be keyed up to surpass previous records or to attain some fixed standard.

To ascertain to what extent the principle of competition was consciously employed by business firms and what methods were used to apply it in increasing the efficiency of the men, a number of successful business firms were asked the following questions:—

How do you utilize competition in increasing efficiency among your employees?

(1) Do you regard it as unwise to stimulate competition in any form? <p 59>

(2) Do you encourage men to excel their own records of previous years?

(3) Do you encourage competition between men in the same department?

(4) Do you encourage competition between your own departments?

(5) Do you encourage competition with departments of competing establishments?

(6) In competition do you make it fair by ``handicapping" your men?

What reward does the winner receive, e.g.:—

(1) Monetary reward?

(2) Promotion?

(3) Public commendation?

In answers by equally successful managers great diversity of opinion prevailed. Some men were afraid of all forms of competition.

They believed that co<o:>peration was essential to success and that any form of competition among the men tended to lessen such co<o:>peration. Most of the men interviewed believed that competition when wisely handled is very effective in stimulating the men.

Of course, most firms try in some way to <p 60> encourage their men to excel their record of previous years. The inquiry developed, however, that a few are unwilling to employ competition even in this mild form as a means to increased efficiency. Most of the firms made conscious use of this principle and were convinced of its potency.

Competition between men in the same department was approved by a majority of the firms, and its adaptability to the selling department was especially emphasized. But some of the best houses will permit no such competition. The diversity in opinion was very pronounced in answering this question.

As to encouraging competition between departments in the same firm, no general answer is satisfactory. Organizations differ widely. In many houses such competition is not practicable; in others it certainly is not to be encouraged. In many organizations which would admit of such competition the experiment had not been tried. In others it has become a regular practice and is looked upon with favor.

In competition between members of the <p 61> same department or between departments the danger of jealousy and enmity seems to be so real that the greatest caution has to be observed in managing the contests. When such caution is exercised, the results are ordinarily reported upon favorably.

As to encouraging competition with departments of rival establishments, the diversity of business makes general statements un- illuminating. Even where such a course is possible, some managers reject the practice as unwise. They believe that it is not best to recognize other houses or to consider them in this particular. A few firms report that they are able to stimulate their men successfully in this way, even though the conditions for such a contest are difficult to handle. Of those who utilize competition a few houses employ no handicaps to put their men on the same level and make success equally possible to all.

The principle of handicaps is so manifestly fair that organizers of contests can hardly afford to neglect this essential to the widest interest and participation in the competition. <p 62>

If the little man in a country territory doesn't feel that he has a fighting chance to equal or surpass the man in the big agency, he makes no attempt to qualify. And the purpose of every contest, of course, is to get every man into the game.

Touching monetary rewards for the winners, there is practical unanimity of opinion. The winner should receive a prize in cash or its equivalent. Usually the effort is to distribute the prizes so that all who excel their average records receive compensation and recognition for the additional work. In many instances unusual increases in sales or output are rewarded by a higher rate of compensation.

That success in contests should influence promotion was generally agreed. The knowledge and energy shown are indications of capacity to occupy a better position.

The contest merely reveals such capacity; the promotion might well follow as part of the prize for the winner or winners.

Public commendation of winners in com- <p 63> petitions is held by many firms to be bad policy. There is fear that such commendation might render the participant conceited and unfit for further usefulness. A majority of firms, however, give the widest possible publicity to such commendation. This, indeed, is the reward most generally used and apparently most keenly desired by employees. Reproduction of photographs of the winners in the house organ with an account of their achievements is the commonest acknowledgment of their success, though posting the names of the winners in various parts of the establishment is the method employed by smaller houses.

Many important houses use competition as part of their regular equipment for handling and energizing men.

Particularly is this true of manufacturers and distributors of specialties, patented machines, trade-marked goods and lines, and wholesalers whose travelers are selling in territories where conditions are generally the same. Several firms of this sort make con- <p 64> scious and elaborate use of the instinct of competition in their ordinary scheme of management.

A concrete and typical illustration of its application to selling is afforded by the experience and the undoubted success of one of the largest specialty houses which distributes its products direct to the consumer. The sales force numbers about 500 men, and executives of wide experience declare that the organization is, of its size, the most efficient in the United States. Analysis of this company's methods is most illuminating and suggestive because every phase of the instinct of competition has been exploited to the advantage of both the house and its employees.

The medium of competition is a series of contests—monthly, quarterly, even yearly which bring into play all the motives urging individuals to maximum effort and industry desire to beat bogy, ambition to win in individual contest with immediate neighbors and against the whole organization, team spirit in <p 63> the matching of one group of agencies against another group, and finally organization spirit in the battle of the whole force to equal or surpass the mark which has been set for it.

The first and basic contest here is that of the individual salesman against his bogy or ``sales quota."

This quota, the monthly amount of business which each agency should produce, has been worked out with great care and has a scientific foundation. Since the great bulk of sales are made to retail merchants, the possibilities of each territory are determined by reckoning the total population of all towns containing three retailers rated by commercial agencies. For normal months there is a standard quota, a little above the monthly average of all agencies the previous year, reckoned against their total urban populations. In ``rush" months, this quota is advanced from fifteen to forty per cent, as the judgment of the sales manager dictates. If general and trade conditions lead him to believe, for instance, that the month of May should produce <p 66> $1,000,000 in orders, while the sum of the usual quotas is $800,000, he calls for an over- plus of twenty per cent. The territory containing one per cent of the total urban population of the country, as reckoned, would then be expected to make sales equal to $10,000. This would be the agency quota for the month, and the first and most important task of the agent would be to secure it.

Because all quotas, both normal and special, are figured on the productive population of the territories and standings may be calculated by percentages, it follows that all agents are on terms of equality.

This is essential in a contest for individual leadership as well as in team or organization matches. For at least eight months of the year, there is such a competition for the best selling record in the entire force. Variety is given to these contests and the interest of the men sustained by changing the terms of the competition. One month the chief prize will be given to the salesman who secures his quota at the earliest date; next month the <p 67> award will be for the individual who first obtains a fixed sum in orders, usually $2500; leadership the third month will go to the man who gets the highest per cent of his quota during the entire period; again, the honor will fall to the agent whose net sales total the greatest for the month.

Further changes are rung and the inspirational effect of the contest immensely increased by enlarging the conditions so that every third or fourth agent is able to qualify for the month's honors and a prize.

Here, for instance, besides the prize for the first agent selling $2500, there will be prizes—like hats, umbrellas, and so on—for every man who closes $2500 in orders before the twentieth of the month, with the attendant publicity of having his portrait and his record printed in the house organ which goes to every agent in the field and every department and executive at the factory. Before leaving the individual contests, mention should be made of the ``star" club of agents who sell $30,000 or more during the year; the presi- <p 68> dency going to the agent who first secures that total, the other official positions falling to his nearest rivals in the order in which they finish.

The team and organization contests are usually carried on simultaneously with the individual competitions. These range from matches between the forces of the big city offices, like New York, Chicago, and St. Louis, upward to district contests in which each team represents from thirty to fifty salesmen and finally to international ``wars" where the American organization is pitted against all the agents abroad. Challenges from one district to another usually precipitate the district competitions; once a year there is a three months' general contest in which all the districts take part for the championship of the whole selling force.

To announce contests is a simple matter; to organize and execute them so that they are of benefit is much more difficult.

Unless the interest of the men is focused on the contests, they are not worth while. To <p 69> make them successful the firm under consideration utilized the following devices:—

During the contest the house organ appeared often and was devoted almost exclusively to the contest. In it the record of each salesman was printed, his quota, his sales to date, and other pertinent information. The sheet was edited by a ``sporting editor," and great tact and skill were displayed in giving the contest the atmosphere of an actual race or game. In addition the sales manager, the district managers, and the house executives wrote letters and telegrams of encouragement, and even made trips to the agencies that got under way too slowly.

The unique feature of the contest was the manner in which the ``sporting editor" gave actuality to the contests by pictorial representations. One competition took the form of a shooting match. The house organ contained an enormous target with two rings and a bull's eye. When a salesman qualified with orders for $625, he was credited with a shot inside the outer ring and his name was <p 70> printed there. With $1250 in sales, he moved into the inner ring, and when his orders amounted to $2500, he was credited with a bull's eye and his name blazoned in the center space.

Another contest was represented as a balloon race between the different districts. Each district was given a balloon, and as sales increased, the airship mounted higher. On the balloon the name of the district leader in sales was printed, while cartoons enlivened the race by showing the expedients, in terms of orders, by which the district managers and their crews sought to drive their airships higher. Each issue of the house organ showed the current standing of the districts by the heights of their balloons.

This conception of the selling contest was very successful. ``Going up—going up—how far are you up now?" was used as a call, and it seemed to strike the men and inspire them. It became the greeting of the salesmen when they met, and irresistibly produced a feeling of competition and a desire to have the district balloon go higher. <p 71>

Other ingenious fancies by which the contests were given the appeal and interest of popular sports was their conception as a baseball game, a football game, an automobile race, a Marathon run, and so on.

In providing prizes, the firm was rather generous, though the expense was never great. While the contest was in progress, all those who were really ``in the running" had the satisfaction of honorable mention, with their photographs reproduced in the house bulletin. This honor and publicity was the chief reward received by the great majority of contestants, and was adequate. Minor prizes were offered on conditions, allowing a large number to qualify, and tempting virtually everybody to make an effort to win one. The value of the prizes did not need to be great, for each man was impressed with the idea that his comrades were watching him, that they observed every advance or retrogression. Success in the contest meant ``making good" in the eyes of the other salesmen as well as in the eyes of his superiors. <p 72>

This desire for social approval and the spirited comment of the editor had a marked influence on the efficiency of many of the younger salesmen.

These special contests were conducted chiefly during the ``rush" seasons, when activity and efficiency of salesmen meant greater returns to the house. Because of their varied forms the contests did not become monotonous, and thus fail in their effect. During the three or four ``big" selling months when special quotas were announced, an individual pocket schedule was mailed to each man, showing how much business he must close each day to keep pace with ``Mr. Quota," the constant competitor.

The most industrious and ambitious men are stimulated by competition; with the less industrious such a stimulation is often wonder working in its effects.

For many positions in the business world a hypothetical bogy should be created after the style of the quota referred to above.

To increase the feeling of comradeship and <p 73> promote co<o:>peration between the men the entire organization or single sections of it occasionally should be made the unit of competition. This is perhaps the most helpful form of competition, but it is hard to execute.

Valuable prizes should always be given to the winners. This ``need" may not necessarily be monetary.

Promotion should not depend upon success in contests, but such success may be well reckoned in awarding promotions.

Public commendation for success in competition costs the company little and is greatly appreciated by the winner. There seems to be no reason why the head of the house should not assist in the presentation.

The most essential factor in creating interest in a contest is the skill of the ``sporting editor" in injecting the real spirit of the game into each contest, thus securing wide publicity, and enlisting the co<o:>peration of large numbers of participants.

Prizes should be widely distributed, so that the greatest number may be encouraged. <p 74>

A fair system of handicapping should be adopted in every case where equal opportunity to win is not possessed by all. Previous records often make successful bogies, and should be more extensively employed.

It is possible to carry on contests between individuals in the same department without jealousies, but skill is required to conduct them. There is the danger that individuals will seek to win by hindering others as well as by exerting themselves. Where it is not possible to carry on a contest and retain a feeling of comradeship between the men, no competition should be encouraged.

CHAPTER IV

LOYALTY

AS A MEANS OF INCREASING HUMAN EFFICIENCY

DELAYED by a train of accidents, a big contractor faced forfeiture of his bond on a city tunnel costing millions of dollars. He had exhausted his ingenuity and his resources to comply with the terms of his contract, but had failed. Because public opinion had been condemning concessions on other jobs on flimsy grounds, the authorities refused to extend the time allowed for completing the work. By canceling the contract, collecting the penalty, and reletting the task, the city would profit without exceeding its legal rights.

In his dilemma, he called his foremen together and explained the situation to them. ``Tell the men," he said. Many of these <p 75> <p 76> had been members of his organization for years, moving with him from one undertaking to the next, looking to him for employment, for help in dull seasons or in times of misfortune, repaying him with interest in their tasks and a certain rough attachment.

He had been unusually considerate, adopting every possible safeguard for their protection, recognizing their union, employing three shifts of men, paying more than the required scale when conditions were hard or dangerous.

A score of unions were represented in the organization: miners, masons, carpenters, plasterers, engineers, electricians, and many grades of helpers. Learning his plight, they rallied promptly to his aid. They appealed to their trades and to the central body of unions to intervene in his behalf with the city officials.

How One Considerate Employer was protected by his Men

As taxpayers, voters, and members of an organization potentially effective in politics, <p 77> they approached the mayor and the department heads concerned. They pointed out— what was true—that the city's negligence in prospecting and charting the course of the tunnel was partly responsible for the contractor's failure. They pleaded that the city should make allowances rather than interrupt their employment, and that the delay in the work would counterbalance any advantage contingent on forfeiture. They promised also that if three additional months were given the contractor, they would *do all in their power to push construction.*

The mayor yielded; the extension was granted. And the men made their promise good literally, waiving jealously guarded rights and sparing no effort to forward the undertaking. The miners, masons, carpenters, and specialists in other lines in which additional skilled men could not be secured labored frequently in twelve-hour shifts and accepted only the regular hourly rate for the overtime. With such zeal animating them, only one conclusion was possible. The tunnel was entirely <p 78> completed before the ninety days of grace had expired.

Here was loyalty as stanch and effective as that which wins battlefields and creates nations. It increased the efficiency of the individual workers; it greatly augmented the effectiveness of the organization as a whole. It was developed, without appeal to sentiment, under conditions which make for division rather than co<o:>peration between employer and employee. The men were unionists; wages, hours, and so on, were contract matters with the boss. Yet in an emergency, the tie between the tunnel builder and his men was strong enough to stand the strain of the fatiguing and long-continued effort necessary to complete the job and save the former from ruin. Like incidents, on perhaps a smaller and less dramatic scale, are not uncommon; but the historian of business has not yet risen to make them known.

<p 79> *Loyalty, to Nation or Organization, shows itself in an Emergency*

As with patriotism, business loyalty needs some such crisis as this to evoke its expression. In peace the patriotism of citizens is rarely evident and is frequently called in question. In America we sometimes assume that it is a virtue belonging only to past generations. But every time the honor or integrity of the country is threatened, a multitude of eager citizens volunteer in its defense. Likewise, many a business man who has come to think his workmen interested only in the wages he pays them, discovers in his hour of need an unsuspected asset in their devotion to the welfare of the business, and their willingness to make sacrifices to bring it past the cape of storms.

Study of any field, of any single house, or of any of the periods of depression which have afflicted and corrected our industrial progress, will convince one of the unfailing and genuine loyalty of men to able and considerate em- <p 80> ployers. So generally true is this, indeed, that ``house patriotism," ``organization spirit," or ``loyalty to the management" is accepted by all great executives as one of the essential elements in the day-by-day conduct of their enterprises.

Striking exhibitions of this loyalty may wait for an emergency. Unless it exists, however, unless it is apparent in the daily routine, there is immediate and relentless search for the antagonistic condition or method, which is robbing the force of present efficiency and future power. Co<o:>peration of employees is the first purpose of organization. Without loyalty and team work the higher levels in output, quality, and service are impossible.

Loyalty on Part of Employer begets Loyalty in his Workers

The importance of loyalty in business could not readily be overestimated, even though its sole function were to secure united action on the part of the officers and men. Where no two men or groups of men were working to <p 81> counter purposes, but all are united in a common purpose, the gain would be enormous, even though the amount of energy put forth by the individuals was not increased in the least. When to this fact of value in organized effort we add the accompanying psychological facts of increased efficiency by means of loyalty, we then begin to comprehend what it means to have or to lack loyalty.

The amount of work accomplished by an individual is subject to various conditions. The whole intellect, feeling, and will must work in unity to secure the best results. Where there is no heart in the work (absence of feeling) relatively little can be accomplished, even though the intellect be convinced and the will strained to the utmost. The employee who lacks loyalty to his employer can at least render but half-hearted service even though he strive to his utmost and though he be convinced that his financial salvation is dependent upon efficient service. *The employer who secures the loyalty of his men not only secures better service, but he enables his men to* *accomplish <p 82> more with less effort and less exhaustion.* The creator of loyalty is a public benefactor.

Such loyalty is always reciprocal. The feeling which workmen entertain for their employer is usually a reflection of his attitude towards them. Fair wages, reasonable hours, working quarters and conditions of average comfort and healthfulness, and a measure of protection against accident are now no more than primary requirements in a factory or store. Without them labor of the better, more energetic types cannot be secured in the first place or held for any length of time. And the employer who expects, in return for these, any more than the average of uninspired service is sure to be disappointed.

If he treats his men like machines, looks at them merely as cogs in the mechanism of his affairs, they will function like machines or find other places. If he wishes to stir the larger, latent powers of their brains and bodies, thereby increasing their efficiency as thinkers and workers, he must recognize them as men and individuals and give in <p 83> some measure what he asks. He must identify them with the business, and make them feel that they have a stake in its success and that the organization has an interest in the welfare of its men. The boss to whom his employees turn in any serious perplexity or private difficulty for advice and aid is pretty apt to receive more than the contract minimum of effort every day and is sure of devoted service in any time of need.

The Effect of Personal Relations in creating Loyalty in a Force

It is on this personal relationship, this platform of mutual interests and helpfulness, that the success and fighting strength of many one- man houses are built. As in the contractor's dilemma already cited, it bears fruit in the fighting zeal, the keener interest, and the extra speed and effort which workers bring to bear on their individual and collective tasks. All the knowledge and skill they possess are thrown into the scale; their quickened intelligences reach out for new methods and short <p 84> cuts; when the crisis has passed, there may be a temporary reaction, but there is likely to be a permanent advance both in individual efficiency and organization spirit.

On the employer's side, this feeling is expressed in the surrender of profits to provide work in dull seasons; in the retention of aged mechanics, laborers, or clerks on the payroll after their usefulness has passed; in pensions; in a score of neighborly and friendly offices to those who are sick, injured, or in trouble. A reputation for ``taking care of his men" has frequently been a bulwark of defense to the small manufacturer or trader assailed by a greedy larger rival.

Personality is, beyond doubt, the primitive wellspring of loyalty. Most men are capable of devotion to a worthy leader; few are ever zealots for the sake of a cause, a principle, a party, or a firm. All these are too abstract to win the affection of the average man. It is only when they become embodied in an individual, a concrete personality which stirs our human interest, that they become moving <p 85> powers. The soldiers of the Revolution fought for Washington rather than for freedom; Christians are loyal to Christ rather than to his teachings; the voter cheers his candidate and not his party; the employee is loyal to the head of the house or his immediate foreman and not to the generality known as the House. Loyalty to the individuals constituting the firm may ultimately develop into house loyalty. To attempt to create the latter sentiment, however, except by first creating it for the men higher up is to go contrary to human nature—always an unwise expenditure of energy.

Human Sympathy as a Factor in developing Loyalty in Men

In developing loyalty, human sympathy is the greatest factor. If an executive of a company is confident that his directors approve his policies, appreciate his obstacles, and are ready to back him up in any crisis, his energy and enthusiasm for the common object never flag. If department heads and <p 86> foremen are assured that the manager is watching their efforts with attention and regard, approving, supporting, and sparing them wherever possible, they will anticipate orders, assume extra burdens, and fling themselves and their forces into any breach which may threaten their chief's program.

If a workman, clerk, or salesman knows that his immediate chief is interested in him personally, that he understands what service is being rendered and is anxious to forward his welfare as well as that of the house, there is no effort, inconvenience, or discomfort which he will not undertake to complete a task which the boss has undertaken. Throughout the entire organization, the sympathy and co<o:>peration of the men above with the men below is essential for securing the highest degree of loyalty. No assumed or manufactured sympathy, however, will take the place of the genuine article.

<p 87> *Personal Relationship with Workers as Basis for creating Loyalty*

The effectiveness of human sympathy in creating loyalty is most apparent in one-man businesses where the head of the house is in personal contact with all or many of his employees. This personal touch, however, is not necessarily limited to the small organization. Many men have employed thousands and secured it. Others have succeeded in impressing their personalities, and demonstrating their sympathy upon large forces, though their actual relations were with a few. The impression made upon these and the loyalty created in them were sufficient to permeate and influence the entire body. Potter Palmer, the elder Armour, Marshall Field, and Andrew

Carnegie were among the hundreds of captains who made acquaintance with the men in the ranks the cornerstone on which they raised their trade or industrial citadels.

When the size of the organization precludes personal contact, or when conditions remove <p 88> the executive to a distance, the task of maintaining touch is frequently and successfully intrusted to a lieutenant in sympathy with the chief's ideals and purposes. He may be the head of a department variously styled, —adjustments, promotion and discharge, employment, labor,—but his express function is to restore to an organization the simple but powerful human relation without which higher efficiency cannot be maintained. In factories and stores employing many women this understudy to the manager is usually a woman, who is given plenary authority in the handling of her charges, in reviewing disputes with foremen, and in finding the right position for the misplaced worker. Whether man or woman, this representative of the manager hears all grievances, reviews all discharges, reductions, and the like, and makes sure that the employee receives a little more than absolute justice.

Many successful merchants and manufacturers, however, disdain agents and intermediaries in this relation and are always ac- <p 89> cessible to every man in their organizations; holding that, since the co<o:>peration of employees is the most important single element in business, the time given to securing it is time well spent.

Even though human sympathy may well be regarded as the most important consideration in increasing loyalty, it is not sufficient in and of itself. The most patriotic citizens are those who have, served the state. They are made loyal by the very act of service. They have assumed the responsibility of promoting the welfare of the state, and their patriotism is thereby stimulated and given concrete outlet. A paternalistic government in which the citizens had every right but no responsibility would develop beggars rather than patriots.

Similarly in a business house ideally organized to create loyalty, each employee not only feels that his rights are protected, but also feels a degree of responsibility for the success and for the good name of the house. He feels that his task or process is an essen- <p 90> tial part of the firm's activity; and hence is important and worthy of his best efforts. To cement this bond and make closer the identification of the employee with the house many firms encourage their employees to purchase stock in the company. Others have worked out profit-sharing plans by which their men share in the dividends of the good years and are given a powerful incentive to promote teamwork and the practice of the economies from which the overplus of profit is produced.

Loyalty may be developed by Education in House History and Policies

The stability of a nation depends on the patriotism of its citizens. Among methods for developing this patriotism, *education* ranks as the most effective. In the public schools history is taught for the purpose of awakening the love and loyalty of the rising generations. The founders, builders, and saviors of the country, the great men of peace and war who have contributed to its advancement, are held up for admiration. From the recital of what <p 91> country and patriotism meant to Washington, Jefferson, Lincoln, Grant, and a host of lesser heroes, the pupils come to realize what country should, and does, mean to them. They become patriotic citizens.

Grounding the New Employee in Company Traditions and Ideals

In like manner the history of any house can be used to inspire loyalty and enthusiasm among its employees. Business has not been slow to borrow the methods and ideals of education, but the writer has been unable to discover any company which makes adequate use of this principle. That this loyalty may be directed to the house as a whole, and not merely to immediate superiors, every employee should be acquainted with the purposes and policies of the company and should understand that the sympathy which he discovers in his foreman is a common characteristic of the whole organization, clear up to the president. The best way to teach this is by example— by incidents drawn from the past, or by a <p 92> review of the development of the company's policy.

To identify one's self with a winning cause, party, or leader, also, is infinitely easier than to be loyal to a loser. For this reason the study of the history of the firm may well include its trade triumphs, past and present; the remarkable or interesting uses to which its products have been put; the honor or prestige which its executives or members of the organization have attained; and the hundred other items of human interest which can be marshaled to give it house personality. All this would arouse admiration and appreciation in employees, would stir enthusiasm and a desire to contribute to future achievements, and would foster an unwillingness to leave the organization.

Some companies have begun in this direction. New employees, by way of introduction, listen to lectures, either with or without the accompaniment of pictures, which review what the house has accomplished, define its standing in the trade, analyze its products and <p 93> their qualities or functions, sketch the plan and purpose of its organization, and touch upon the other points of chief human interest. Other companies put this information in booklets. Still others employ their house organs to recall and do honor to the interesting traditions of the company as well as to exploit the successful deeds and men of the moment. An organized and continuous campaign of education along this line should prove an inexpensive means of increasing loyalty and efficiency among the men. To the mind of the writer, it seems clear that the future will see pronounced advances in this particular.

Personality can be overdone, however. Workers instinctively give allegiance to strong, balanced men, but resent and combat egotism unchecked by regard for others' rights. Exploitation of the employer's or foreman's personality will do more harm than good unless attended by consideration for the personality of the employee. The service of more than one important company has been made intolerable for men of spirit and creative ability <p 94> by the arrogant and dominating spirit of the management. The men who continue to sacrifice their individuality to the whim or the arbitrary rule of their superiors, in time lose their ambition and initiative; and the organization declines to a level of routine, mechanical efficiency only one remove from dry- rot.

How Efficiency and Loyalty of Workers may be Capitalized

Conservation and development of individuality in workers may be made an important factor in creating loyalty as well as in directly increasing efficiency. Great retail stores put many department heads into business for themselves, giving them space, light, buying facilities, clerks, and purchasing and advertising credit as a basis of their merchandising; then requiring a certain percentage of profit on the amount allowed them. The more successful of Marshall Field's lieutenants were taken into partnership and, as in the case of Andrew Carnegie and his ``cabinet of young <p 95> geniuses," were given substantial shares of the wealth they helped to create.

Some industries and stores carry this practice to the point of making specialized departments entirely independent of the general buying, production, and selling organizations whenever these fall short of the service offered outside; while the principle of stock distribution or other forms of profit sharing has been adopted by so many companies that it has come to be a recognized method of promoting loyalty.

Regard for the employee's personality must be carried down in an unbroken chain through all the ranks. It may be broken at any step in the descent by an executive or foreman who has not himself learned the lesson that loyalty to the house includes loyalty to the men under him.

It is not uncommon, in some American houses, to find three generations of workers —grandfather, father, and apprentice son— rendering faithful and friendly service; or to discover a score of bosses and men who have <p 96> spent thirty or forty years—their entire productive lives—in the one organization. Where such a bond exists between employer and employees, it becomes an active, unfailing force in the development of loyalty, not only among the veterans, but also among the newest recruits for whom it realizes an illustration of what true co<o:>peration means.

Many Examples of the Loyalty of Executives for their Men in Danger

This double loyalty—to the chief and to the organization—is not a plant of slow growth. Few mine accidents or industrial disasters occur without bringing to merited, but fleeting, fame some heroic superintendent or lesser boss who has risked his own life to save his men or preserve the company's property. The same sense of responsibility extends to every grade. Give a man the least touch of authority and he seems to take on added moral stature. The engineer who clings to his throttle with collision imminent has his counterparts in the ``handy man" <p 97> who braves injury to slip a belt and save another workman or a costly machine, and in the elevator conductor who drives his car up and down through flames and smoke to rescue his fellows. Such efficiency and organization spirit is the result of individual growth as well as the impression of the employer's personality upon his machine.

A Disloyal Sales Manager and his Influence on his Force

On the other hand, lack of loyalty on the part of employers towards their men is almost as common as failing devotion on the part of workers. Too many assume that the mere providing of work and the payment of wages give them the right to absolute fidelity, even when they take advantage of their men. The sales manager concerned in the following incident refused to believe that his attitude towards his men had anything to do with the lack of enthusiasm and low efficiency in his force.

An experienced salesman who had lost his <p 98> position because of the San Francisco fire applied to the sales manager for a position. He was informed that there were fifteen applicants for the Ohio territory, but that the place would be given to him because of his better record. The manager laid out an initial territory in one corner and ordered the salesman to work it first.

Working this territory, the salesman secured substantial orders, but refrained from ``over-selling" any customer, gave considerable time to missionary work and to cultivating the acquaintance of buyers. His campaign was planned less for immediate results than for the future and for the effect on the larger field of the state. Having no instructions as to pushing his wider campaign, in about sixty days he asked for instructions. In answer he was ordered home and discharged on the ground that business was dull and that he had been a loss to the house. During the sixty days he had been working on a losing commission basis with the expectation of taking his profits later. Investigation dis- <p 99> closed that he was but one of five salesmen to whom the Ohio territory had been assigned simultaneously. Of the five, one other also had made good and had been retained because he could be secured for less money.

This multiple try-out policy is entirely fair when the applicants know the conditions. But to lead each applicant to believe that he has been engaged subject only to his ability to make good is manifestly unjust. The facts are bound to come out sooner or later and create distrust among all employees of the house. Loyalty is strictly reciprocal. If an employee feels that he has no assurance of fair treatment, his attitude towards the firm is sure to be negative. Even the man who secures the position will recognize the firm's lack of candor and will never give his employers the full measure of co<o:>peration which produces maximum efficiency.

The ``square deal," indeed, is the indispensable basis of loyalty and efficiency in an organization. The spirit as well as the letter of the bargain must be observed, else the work- <p 100> men will contrive to even up matters by loafing, by slighting the work, or by a minimum production. This means a loss of possible daily earnings. On the other hand, employees never fail to recognize and in time respect the executive who holds the balance of loyalty and justice level between them and the business.

Fair wages, reasonable hours, working quarters and conditions of average comfort and healthfulness, ordinary precautions against accidents, and continuous employment are all now regarded as primary requirements and are not sufficient to create loyalty in the men. More than this must be done.

The chief executive should create such a spirit that his officers shall turn to him for help when in perplexity or difficulty. The superintendent and officers or bosses should sustain this same sympathetic relationship toward their men that the executive has toward his officers. A reputation for taking care of his men is a thing to be sought in a chief executive as well as in all underofficers.

Personal relationships should be cultivated. <p 101> In some large organizations the chief executive may secure this personal touch with individuals through an agent or through a department known as the department of ``promotion and discharge," ``employment," or ``labor." In others, occasional meetings on a level of equality may be brought about through house picnics, entertainments, vacation camps, and so on, where employer and employee meet each other outside their usual business environment.

It is not worth while to attempt to develop loyalty to the house until there has been developed a loyalty to the personalities representing the house. Loyalty in business is in the main a reciprocal relationship. The way to begin it is for the chief to be loyal to his subordinates and to see to it that all officers are loyal to their inferiors. When loyalty from above has been secured, loyalty from the ranks may readily be developed.

The personality of the worker must be respected by the employer. ``Giving a man a chance" to develop himself, allowing him <p 102> to express his individuality, is the surest way of enlisting the interest and loyalty of a creative man.

To identify the interests of employees with the interests of the house, various plans of profit sharing, sale of stock to employees, pensions, insurance against sickness and accident, and so on, have been successfully applied by many companies.

So far as possible, responsibility for the success of the house should be assumed by all employees. In some way the workmen should feel that they are in partnership with the executives. We easily develop loyalty for the cause for which we have taken responsibility or rendered a service.

Creating Loyalty to Firm itself by Educational Campaign

A perpetual campaign of publicity should be maintained for the benefit of every man in the employ of the house. In this there should be a truthful but emphatic presentation of acts of loyalty on the part of either employers or <p 103> workmen. Everything connected with the firm which has human interest should be included in this history. This educational campaign should change the loyalty to the *men in the firm into loyalty to the *firm itself. It should be an attempt to give the firm a personality, and of such a noble character that it would win the loyalty of the men. This could be accomplished at little expense and with great profit.

CHAPTER V

CONCENTRATION

AS A MEANS OF INCREASING HUMAN EFFICIENCY

THE owner of one of the largest and most complex businesses in America handles his day's work on a schedule as exacting as a railway time-table. In no other way could he keep in touch with and administer the manifold activities of his industry and a score of allied interests—buying of the day's raw materials for a dozen plants in half as many markets, direction of an organization exceeding 20,000 men, selling and delivering a multitude of products in a field as wide as three continents, financing the whole tremendous fabric.

Every department of his business, therefore, has its hour or quarter hour in the daily program when its big problems are considered <p 104> <p 105> and settled on the tick of the clock. This schedule is flexible, since no two days bring from any division of production, distribution, or financing the same demands upon the owner's attention. Yet each keeps its place and comes invariably under his eye—through reports and his own mastery of conditions affecting the department.

To secure the high personal efficiency required for this oversight and methodical dispatch of affairs, the owner-executive is not only protected from outside interruptions and distractions, but is also guarded against intrusion of the vital elements of his business—both men and matters — except at the moment most advantageous for dealing with them.

Analysis and organization have determined these moments—just as they have eliminated every non-essential in the things presented for consideration and decision. Except when emergencies arise there is no departure from the rule: ``One thing at a time—the big thing—at the right time." The task in hand is never cheated, or allowed to cheat the next <p 106> in line. Management is as much a continuous process, organized and wasteproof, as the journey of raw materials through his plants.

This is an illustration of remarkable individual efficiency attained by concentration —the power of the human mind which seems inseparable from any great achievement in business, in politics, in the arts, in education. Through it men of moderate capacities have secured results apparently beyond the reach of genius. And in no field has this power of concentration been displayed more vividly by leaders or been more generally lacking in the rank and file than in business. Analysis of the conditions may suggest the reason and the remedy.

The modern business man is exhausted no more by his actual achievements than by the things which he is compelled to resist doing.

Appeals for his attention are ceaseless. The roar of the street, the ring of telephone bells, the din of typewriting machines, the sight of a row of men waiting for an interview, the muffled voices from neighboring offices or <p

107> workers, the plan for the day's work which is being delayed, the anxiety for the results for certain endeavors, suspicion as to the loyalty of employees—these and a score of other distractions are constantly bombarding him.

Every appeal for attention demands expenditure of energy—to ignore it and hold the mind down to the business in hand. The simple life with its single appeal is not for the business man. For him life is complex and strenuous. To overcome distractions and focus his mind on one thing is a large part of his task. If this single thing alone appealed to his attention, the effort would be pleasing and effective. It is not the work that is hard; the strain comes in keeping other things at bay while completing the pressing duty.

He is exhausted, not because of his achievements, but because of the expenditure of energy in resisting distractions.

He is inefficient, not through lack of industry, but from lack of opportunity or of ability to concentrate his energy upon the single task at hand. <p 108>

All sources of illumination—from the candle to the sun—send out rays of light equally in all directions. If illumination of only *one point is desired, the loss is appalling. The rays may be assembled, however, by reflectors and lenses and so brought to bear in great force at a single point.

This brilliancy is not secured by greater expenditure of energy, but by utilizing the rays which, except for the reflectors and lenses, would be dissipated in other directions.

As any source gives off equally in all directions, so the human intellect seems designed to respond to all forms and sorts of appeal for attention.

To keep light from going off in useless directions we use reflectors; to keep human energy from being expended in useless directions we must remove distractions. To focus the light at any point we use lenses; to focus our minds at any point we use concentration.

Concentration is a state secured by the mental activity called attention. To understand concentration we must first consider the more fundamental facts of attention. <p 109>

In the evolution of the human race certain things have been so important for the individual and the race that responses towards them have become instinctive. They appeal to every individual and attract his attention without fail. Thus moving objects, loud sounds, sudden contrasts, and the like, were ordinarily portents of evil to primitive man, and his attention was drawn to them irresistibly. Even for us to pay attention to such objects requires no intention and no effort. Hence it is spoken of as *passive or *involuntary attention.

The attention of animals and of children is practically confined to this passive form, while adults are by no means free from it. For instance, ideas and things to which I have no intention of turning my mind attract me. Ripe fruit, gesticulating men, beautiful women, approaching holidays, and scores of other things simply pop up in my mind and enthrall my attention. My mind may be so concentrated upon these things that I become oblivious to pressing responsibilities. In some <p 110> instances the concentration may be but momentary; in others there may result a day dream, a building of air castles, which lasts for a long time and recurs with distressing frequency.

Such attention is action in the line of least resistance. Though it may suffice for the acts of animals and children it is sadly deficient for our complex business life.

Even here, however, it is easy to relapse to the lower plane of activity and to respond to the appeal of the crier in the street, the inconvenience of the heat, the news of the ball game, or a pleasing reverie, or even to fall into a state of mental apathy. The warfare against these distractions is never wholly won. Banishing these allurements results in the concentration so essential for successfully handling business problems. The strain is not so much in solving the problems as in retaining the concentration of the mind.

When an effort of will enables us to overcome these distractions and apply our minds to the subject in hand, the strain soon repeats itself. <p 111> It frequently happens that this struggle is continuous—particularly when the distractions are unusual or our physical condition is below the normal. No effort of the will is able to hold our minds down to work for any length of time unless the task develops interest in itself.

This attention with effort is known as *voluntary attention. It is the most exhausting act which any individual can perform. Strength of will consists in the power to resist distractions and to hold the mind down to even the most uninteresting occupations.

Fortunately for human achievement, acts which in the beginning require voluntary effort may later result without effort.

The schoolboy must struggle to keep his mind on such uninteresting things as the alphabet. Later he may become a literary man and find that nothing attracts his attention so quickly as printed symbols. In commercial arithmetic the boy labors to fix his attention on dollar signs and problems involving profit and loss. Launched in business, <p 112> however, these things may attract him more than a football game.

It is the outcome of previous application that we now attend without effort to many things in our civilization which differ from those of more primitive life. Such attention without effort is known as *secondary passive attention*. Examples are furnished by the geologist's attention to the strata of the earth, the historian's to original manuscripts, the manufacturer's to by-products, the merchant's to distant customers, and the attention which we all give to printed symbols and scores of other things unnoticed by our distant ancestors. Here our attention is similar to passive attention, though the latter was the result of inheritance, while our secondary passive attention results from our individual efforts and is the product of our training.

Through passive attention my concentration upon a ``castle in Spain'' may be perfect until destroyed by a fly on my nose. Voluntary attention may make my concentration upon the duty at hand entirely satisfactory <p 113> till dissipated by some one entering my office. Secondary passive attention fixes my mind upon the adding of a column of figures, and it may be distracted by a commotion in my vicinity. Thus concentration produced by any form of attention is easily destroyed by a legion of possible disturbances. If I desire to increase my concentration to the maximum, I must remove every possible cause of distraction.

Organized society has recognized the hindering effect of some distractions and has made halting attempts to abolish them.

Thus locomotives are prohibited from sounding whistles within city limits, but power plants are permitted by noise and smoke to annoy every citizen in the vicinity. Street cars are forbidden to use flat wheels, but are still allowed to run on the surface or on a resounding structure and thus become a public nuisance. Steam calliopes, newsboys, street venders, and other unnecessary sources of noise are still tolerated.

In the design and construction of office <p 114> buildings, stores, and factories in noisy neighborhoods, too little consideration is given to existing means of excluding or deadening outside sounds, though the newer office buildings are examples of initiative in this direction; not only are they of sound-proof construction, but in many instances they have replaced the noisy pavements of the streets with blocks which reduce the clatter to a minimum. In both improvements they have been emulated by some of the great retail stores which have shut out external noises and reduced those within to a point where they no longer distract the attention of clerks or customers from the business of selling and buying. In many, however, clerks are still forced to call aloud for cash girls or department managers, and the handling of customers at elevators is attended by wholly unnecessary shouting and clash of equipment.

Of all distractions, sound is certainly the most common and the most insistent in its appeal.

The individual efforts towards reducing it quoted above were stimulated by the hope <p 115> of immediate and tangible profit—sound- proof offices commanding higher rents and quiet stores attracting more customers. In not a few cases, manufacturers have gone deeper, however, recognizing that anything which claims the attention of an employee from his work reduces his efficiency and cuts profits, even though he be a piece worker. In part this explains the migration of many industries to the smaller towns and the development of a new type of city factory with sound- proof walls and floors, windows sealed against noise, and a system of mechanical ventilation.

The individual manufacturer or merchant, therefore, need not wait for a general crusade to abate the noise, the smoke, and the other distractions which reduce his employee's effectiveness. In no small measure he can shut out external noises and eliminate many of those within. Loud dictation, conversations, clicking typewriters, loud-ringing telephones, can all be cut to a key which makes them virtually indistinguishable in an office of any size. More and more the big open office as <p 116> an absorbent of sound seems to be gaining in favor. In one of the newest and largest of these I know, nearly all the typewriting machines are segregated in a glass-walled room, and long-distance telephone messages can be taken at any instrument in the great office.

Like sound in its imperative appeal for attention is the consciousness of strangers passing one's desk or windows.

Movement of fellow employees about the department, unless excessive or unusual, is hardly noticed; let an individual or a group with whom we are not acquainted come within the field of our vision, and they claim attention immediately. For this reason shops or factories whose windows command a busy street find it profitable to use opaque glass to shut out the shifting scene.

This scheme of retreat and protection has been carried well-nigh to perfection by many executives. Private offices guarded by secretaries fortify them against distractions and unauthorized claims on their attention, both from within and without their organizations. <p 117> Routine problems, in administration, production, distribution, are never referred to them; these are settled by department heads, and only new or vital questions are submitted to the executive. In many large companies, besides the department heads and secretaries who assume this load of routine, there are assistants to the president and the general manager who further reduce the demands upon their chiefs. The value of time, the effect of interruptions and distractions upon their own efficiency, are understood by countless executives who neglect to guard their employees against similar distractions.

Individual business men, unsupported by organizations, have worked out individual methods of self-protection.

One man postpones consideration of questions of policy, selling conditions, and soon until the business of the day has been finished, and interruptions from customers or employees are improbable. Another, with his stenographer, reaches his office half an hour earlier than his organization, and, picking out the day's big <p 118> task, has it well towards accomplishment before the usual distractions begin. The foremost electrical and mechanical engineer in the country solves his most difficult and abstruse problems at home, at night. His organization provides a perfect defense against interruptions; but only in the silence, the isolation of his home at night, does he find the complete absence of distraction permitting the absolute concentration which produces great results.

This chapter was prefaced by an instance where protection from distractions through organization was joined with methodical attack on the elements of the day's work. This combination approaches the ideal; it is the system followed by nearly all the great executives of America. Time and attention are equably allotted to the various interests, the various departments of effort which must have the big man's consideration during the day. Analysis has determined how much of each is required; appointments are made with the men who must co<o:>perate; all other matters are pushed aside until a decision is reached; <p 119> and upon the completion of each attention is concentrated on the next task.

A striking instance of this organization of work and concentration upon a single problem is afforded by the ``cabinet meetings'' of some large corporations and the luncheons of groups of powerful financiers in New York. There are certain questions to be settled, a definite length of time in which to settle them. In the order of their importance they are allotted so many minutes. At the expiration of that time a vote is taken, the president or chairman announces his decision, and the next matter is attacked.

There is no royal method of training in concentration. It is in the main developed by repeated acts of attention upon the subject in hand.

If I am anxious or need to develop the power of concentration upon what people say, either in conversation or in public discourse, I may be helped by persistently and continuously forcing myself to attend. The habit of concentration may to a degree be thus acquired; <p 120> pursuing it, I should never allow myself to listen indifferently, but I must force myself to strict attention.

Such practice would result ultimately in a habit of concentration upon what I hear, but would not necessarily increase my power of concentration upon writing, adding, or other activities. Specific training in each is essential, and even then the results will be far short of what might be desired. Persistent effort in any direction is not without result, however, and any increase in concentration is so valuable that it is worth the effort it costs. If a man lacks power of concentration in any particular direction, he should force concentration in that line and continue till a habit results.

Our control over our muscles and movements far exceeds our direct control over our attention. An attitude of concentration is possible, even when the desired mental process is not present. Thus by fixing my eyes on a page and keeping them adjusted for reading, even when my mind is on a subject far removed, I can help my will to secure concentration. I <p 121> can likewise restrain myself from picking up a newspaper or from chatting with a friend when it is the time for concentrated action on my work. By continuously resisting movements which tend to distract and by holding myself in the position of attention, the strain upon my will in forcing concentration becomes less.

Concentration is practically impossible when the brain is fagged or the bodily condition is far below the normal in any respect.

The connection between the body and the mind is most intimate, and the perfect working of the body is necessary to the highest efficiency of the mind. The power of concentration is accordingly affected by surroundings in the hours of labor, by sleep and recreation, by the quality and quantity of food, and by every condition which affects the bodily processes favorably.

Recognition of this truth is behind the very general movement, both here and abroad, to provide the best possible conditions both in the factories and the home environment of workers. Employers are coming more and more to un- <p 122> derstand that conservation of physical forces means maximum output. The foundation, of course, is a clean, spacious, well-lighted, and perfectly ventilated factory in a situation which affords pure air and accessibility to the homes of employees. In England and Germany the advance towards this ideal has taken form in the ``garden cities'' of which the plant is the nucleus and the support. In America there is no lack of industrial towns planned and built as carefully as the works to which they are tributary.

Some have added various ``welfare'' features, ranging from hot luncheons served at cost, free baths, and medical attendance to night schools for employees to teach them how to live and work to better advantage. The profit comes back in the increased efficiency of the employees.

Even though the health be perfect and the attitude of attention be sustained the will is unable to retain concentration by an effort for more than a few seconds at a time.

When the mind is concentrated upon an <p 123> object, this object must develop and prove interesting, otherwise there will be required every few seconds the same tug of the will. This concentration by voluntary attention is essential, but cannot be permanent. To secure enduring concentration we may have to ``pull ourselves together'' occasionally, but the necessity for such efforts should be reduced. This is accomplished by developing interest in the task before us, through application of the fundamental motives such as self-preservation, imitation, competition, loyalty, and the love of the game.

If the task before me is essential for my self-preservation, I shall find my mind riveted upon it. If I hope to secure more from speculation than from the completion of my present tasks, then my self-preservation is not dependent upon my work and my mind will irresistibly be drawn to the stock market and the race track. If I wish my work to be interesting and to compel my undivided attention, I should then try to make it appeal to me as of more importance than anything <p 124> else in the world. I must be dependent upon it for my income; I must see that others are working and so imitate their action; I must compete with others in the accomplishment of the task; I must regard the work as a service to the house; and I must in every possible way try to ``get into the game."

This conversion of a difficult task into an interesting activity is the most fruitful method of securing concentration.

Efforts of will can never be dispensed with, but the necessity for such efforts should be reduced to the minimum. The assumption of the attitude of attention should gradually become habitual during the hours of work, and so take care of itself.

The methods which a business man must use to cultivate concentration in himself are also applicable to his employees. The manner of applying the methods is, of course, different. The employer may see to it that as far as possible all distractions are removed. He cannot directly cause his men to put forth voluntary effort, but he can see to it that they re- <p 125> tain the attitude of concentration. This may require the prohibition of acts which are distracting but which would otherwise seem indifferent. The employer has a duty in regard to the health of his men. Certain employers have assumed to regulate the lives of their men even after the day's work is over. Bad habits have been prohibited; sanitary conditions of living have been provided; hours of labor have been reduced; vacations have been granted; and sanitary conditions in shop and factory have been provided for.

Employers are finding it to their interest to make concentration easy for their men by rendering their work interesting.

This they have done by making the work seem worth while. The men are given living wages, the hope of promotion is not too long deferred, attractive and efficient models for imitation are provided, friendly competition is encouraged, loyalty to the house is engendered, and love of the work inculcated. In addition, everything which hinders the development of interest in the work has been resisted. <p 126>

How will a salesman, for instance, develop interest in his work if he makes more from his ``side lines'' than from the service he renders to the house which pays his expenses? How can the laborer be interested in his work if he believes that by gambling he can make more in an hour than he could by a month's steady work? The successful shoemaker sticks to his last, the successful professional man keeps out of business, and the wise business man resists the temptation to speculate. Occasionally a man may be capable of carrying on diverse lines of business for himself, but the man is certainly a very great exception who can hold his attention to the interests of his employer when he expects to receive greater rewards from other sources.

The power of concentration depends in part upon inheritance and in part upon training.

Some individuals, like an Edison or a Roosevelt, seem to be constructed after the manner of a searchlight. All their energy may be turned in one direction and all the rest of the world disregarded. Others are what we call scatter- <p 127> brained. They are unable to attend completely to any one thing. They respond constantly to stimulation in the environment and to ideas which seem to ``pop up'' in their minds.

Some people can read a book or paper with perfect satisfaction, even though companions around them are talking and laughing. For others, such attempts are farcical.

Many great men are reputed to have had marvelous powers of concentration. When engaged in their work, they became so absorbed in it that distracting thoughts had no access to their minds, and even hunger, sleep, and salutations of friends have frequently been unable to divert the attention from the absorbing topic.

There are persons who cannot really work except in the midst of excitement.

When surrounded by numerous appeals to attention, they get wakened up by resisting these attractions and find superfluous energy adequate to attend to the subject in hand. This is on the same principle that governs the effects of poisonous stimulants. Taken <p 128> into the system, the whole bodily activity is aroused in an attempt to expel the poison. Some of this abnormally awakened energy may be applied to uses other than those intended by nature. Hence some individuals are actually helped in their work at least temporarily by the use of stimulants. Most of the energy is of course required to expel the poison, and hence the method of generating the energy is uneconomical.

The men who find that they can accomplish the most work and concentrate themselves upon it the most perfectly when in the midst of noise and confusion are paying a great price for the increase of energy, available for profitable work. To be dependent on confusion for the necessary stimulation is abnormal and expensive. Rapid exhaustion and a shortened life result. It is a bad habit and nothing more.

Many persons seem able to disregard the common and necessary distractions of office, store, or factory.

Other persons are so constituted that these distractions can never be overcome. Such <p 129> persons cannot hear a message through a telephone when others in the room are talking; they cannot dictate a letter if a third person is within hearing; they cannot add a column of figures when others are talking. Habit and effort may reduce such disability, but in some instances it will never even approximately eliminate it. Such persons may be very efficient employees, and their inability to concentrate in the presence of distractions should be respected. Every business man is careful to locate every piece of machinery where it will work best, but equal care has not been given to locating men where they may work to the greatest advantage.

By inheritance the power of concentration differs greatly among intelligent persons. By training, those with defective power may improve, but will never perfect the power to concentrate amidst distractions. To subject such persons to distractions is an unwise expenditure of energy

Concentration by voluntary attention should be avoided, but concentration by secondary passive <p 130> attention cultivated. Organized business interests should eliminate such public nuisances as surface street cars, elevated trains, venders of wares, screeching newsboys, smoking chimneys, and the like.

In individual establishments walls may be deadened to sounds, telephones may be muffled, call bells may be replaced by buzzers with indicators, clerks may have other methods than that of calling aloud for ``cash" or for floor walkers, typewriters may be massed with a view to reducing the general commotion, the illumination at the desks may be increased, discomforts should be reduced to a minimum, work may be so systematized that only one task at a time demands attention.

At least the attitude of concentration should be habitual. The bodily condition favorable to the best concentration may make profitable such devices as firm lunch rooms, the building of industrial villages, and so on.

Concentration is secured positively by bringing into activity the various motives which affect most powerfully the different individu- <p 131> als. There should be a universal taboo on horse racing and all forms of gambling. Even ``side lines" should be completely discouraged. Some individuals are so hindered by the ordinary and necessary distractions of business that special protection should be granted to them.

CHAPTER VI

WAGES

AS A MEANS OF INCREASING HUMAN EFFICIENCY

FIFTY years ago works on psychology were devoted largely to discussion of ideas and of concepts. To-day the point of emphasis has changed, and we are now paying much attention to a study of ``attitudes." It is doubtless important to analyze my ideas or concepts, but it is of much more importance to know my attitudes. It is vital to know how to influence the ideas of others; but to be able to influence their attitudes is of still greater significance.

We all know in a general way what we mean by an attitude, but it is difficult to define or to comprehend it exactly. I have one attitude towards a snake and a totally different one towards my students. If when hunting <p 132> <p 133> quail I happen upon a little harmless snake, I find that I respond to the sight in a most absurd manner. Dread and repulsion overcome me. I can hardly restrain myself from killing the snake, even though doing so will frighten the birds I am hunting. I am predisposed to react in a particular way towards a snake. I sustain a particular attitude towards it.

In the presence of my students I find that a spirit of unselfish devotion and a desire to be of assistance are likely to be uppermost. That is to say, I sustain towards my students an attitude of helpfulness, a predisposition to react towards them in such a way that their interests may be furthered. In fact, I find that we all take particular attitudes towards the people we know and towards every task of our lives. These attitudes are very significant, and yet they are often developed by circumstances which made but little apparent impression at the time, or may have been altogether forgotten. I cannot recall, for instance, the experience of my boyhood which developed <p 134> my present absurd attitude toward harmless snakes.

When witnessing a play, my attitude of suspicion towards a particular character may have been promoted by means of music and color, by means of the total setting of the play, or by some other means which never seemed to catch my attention. These concealed agencies threw me into an attitude of suspicion, even while I was not aware that such a result was being attempted.

This modern conception of psychology teaches us that in influencing others we are not successful until we have influenced their attitudes. Children in school do not draw patriotism from mere information about their country. Patriotism comes with the cultivation of the proper attitude towards one's native land.

Success or failure in business is caused more by mental attitude even than by mental capacities.

Nothing but failure can result from the mental attitude which we designate variously as laziness, indifference, indolence, apathy, <p 135> shiftlessness, and lack of interest. All business successes are due in part to the attitudes which we call industry, perseverance, interest, application, enthusiasm, and diligence.

In any individual, too, these attitudes may not be the same towards different objects and may be subject to very profound changes and developments. A schoolboy is frequently lazy when engaged in the study of grammar, but industrious when at work in manual training. A young man who is an indolent bookkeeper may prove to be an indefatigable salesman. Another who has shown himself apathetic and indifferent in a subordinate position may suddenly wake up when cast upon his own responsibility.

Few men of any intelligence can develop the same degree of interest in each of several tasks. Personally I find that my shiftlessness in regard to some of my work is appalling. Touching my main activities, however, I judge that my industry is above reproach.

The preceding chapters (particularly the chapters on Imitation, Competition, and Loy- <p 136> alty) were attempts to discover and to present the most effective motives or factors in producing in workers an attitude of industry. Based on a study of psychology and of business, methods were presented which may be utilized with but little expense and yet are effective in awakening instinctive responses in the worker and hence greatly increasing his efficiency. The present chapter will deal with an even more effective means of securing an attitude of industry since it appeals to three of the most fundamental and irresistible of man's instincts.

With most of us the degree of our laziness or our industry depends partly upon our affinity for the work, but chiefly upon the motives which stimulate us.

For our ancestors, preservation depended upon their securing the necessary means for food, clothing, and shelter. In the struggle for existence only those individuals and races survived who were able to secure these necessary articles. In climates and regions removed from the tropics only the exceedingly <p 137> industrious survived. In warm and fertile lands those who were relatively industrious managed to exist. Because of the absence of the necessity for clothing and because of the abundance of available food, races have developed in the tropics which are notoriously lazy. The human race, individually and collectively, works only where and when it is compelled to.

The energetic races, those which have advanced in civilization, live in lands where the struggle for existence has been continuous. Necessity is a hard master, but its rule is indispensable to worthy achievement. The instinct of self-preservation and the industrious attitude are responses which the human race has learned to exercise, in the main, only in case of need. Self-preservation is the first law; where life and personal liberty are dependent upon industry, idleness will not be found. Wealth removes the obligation to toil; hence the poor boy often outdistances his more favored brother.

Individuals work for pay as a means of <p 138> self-preservation, and unless that is satisfactory other motives have but little weight with them. The needs of the self which preservation demands are continuously increasing. The needs of the American-born laborer are greater than those of the Chinaman. Regardless of this higher standard of living and the ever increasing number of ``necessities," the instinct of self-preservation acts in connection with them all.

Almost without exception the interest of workers centers in the wage. If they could retain their accustomed wage with less effort, they would do so.

If the retention and increase depend on individual production, they will respond to the compulsion.

Every student of psychology recognizes the fact that the wage is more than a means of self-preservation. Man is a distinctly social creature. He has a social self as well as an individual self. His social self demands social approval as much as his individual self demands bread, clothing, and shelter. In our present industrial system this social distinc- <p 139> tion is most often indicated by means of monetary reward. The laborer not only demands that his toil shall provide the means for self- preservation, but he seeks through his wages the social distinction which he feels to be his due. His desire for increase of wages is often partly, and in some instances mainly, due to his craving for distinction or social approval.

In such instances the wage is to be thought of as something comparable to the score of a ball player. The desire for a high score is sufficient motive to beget the most extreme exertion, even though the reward anticipated is nothing more than a sign of distinction and without any relationship whatever to self- preservation.

In common with some of the lower animals man has an instinct to collect and hoard all sorts of things. This instinct is spoken of in psychology as the hoarding or proprietary instinct. In performing instinctive acts we do so with enthusiasm, but blindly. We take great delight in the performing of the act, even though the ultimate result of the act <p 140> may be entirely unknown to us. The squirrel collects and stores nuts with great delight and industry. He has no idea of the approaching winter, but gathers the nuts simply because for him it is the most interesting process in his experience.

Most persons display a like instinctive tendency to make collections and hoard articles. This is particularly apparent in collections of such things as canceled postage stamps, discarded buttons, pebbles, sticks, magazines, and other non-useful articles.

When this hoarding instinct is not controlled by reason or checked by other interests, we have the miser. In a less degree, we all share with the miser his hoarding instinct. We all like to collect money just as the squirrel likes to gather nuts. The octogenarian continues to collect money with unabated zeal, even though he be childless. He is probably not aware that he is collecting merely for the pleasure of collecting.

Since the wage is the means ordinarily employed to awaken in workers the three instincts <p 141> of self-preservation, of social distinction, and of hoarding, it is not strange that an industrial age should regard it as the chief means of increasing efficiency.

The employer has not attempted to discover what instincts were appealed to by the wage, or the most economical method of stimulating these instincts. He has not undervalued the wage in securing efficiency, but rather has assumed that the service secured must be in direct proportion to the amount expended.

Such an assumption is not warranted. Of two employers with equal forces and payrolls one may receive much more and better service than the other. It is not a question merely of how much is spent but how wisely it is spent. The wage secures service to the degree in which it awakens these fundamental instincts under consideration.

It is apparent, therefore, that other factors than the amount of money expended in wages are to be considered by every employer. Without increasing the pay roll he may increase the efficiency of his men. The employer who has <p 142> determined the number of men he needs and the wages he must pay has only begun to solve his labor problem.

In the preparation of the present chapter a large number of business men were interviewed personally or by correspondence.

One of the questions asked was: ``How do you make the most of the wages paid your men?"

As subsidiary to this general question three other questions were asked: ``In paying them do you base the amount to be received by each man upon a fixed salary? By some of the men upon actual output—commissions or piecework rates? By some upon a combination including profit-sharing or bonus?"

The answers to these latter questions were not uniform even among employers engaged apparently in the same business and under very similar conditions. Some reported that all the methods suggested were used in their establishment. Factory hands were employed on piecework or on a premium or bonus basis where conditions permitted; office assistants <p 143> on fixed salaries; department managers upon a combination including profit sharing. The results reported, however, were far from uniform. The astounding feature was the diversity of opinion among successful managers of employees. By various houses one or more of the systems had been tried under apparently favorable conditions and had been discarded. On the other hand each of the systems was advocated by equally successful business firms.

In judging of the relative merits of fixed salaries as compared with other methods the experiences of individual firms offer no certain data. The relative merits and demerits are best disclosed by a psychological analysis of the manner in which the various devices appeal to the employee's instincts and reason.

When wages are based on commission, piece rate, or a bonus or premium system, the stimulus to action is constantly present. Every stroke of the hammer, every sale made, every figure added, increases the wage. The wage thus continuously beckons the worker to greater accomplishment. <p 144>

All other considerations lose in importance, and the mind becomes focused on output. The worker is blinded to all other motives, and invariably sacrifices quality unless this be guarded by rigid inspection. The piecework or task system thus influences the worker directly and incessantly without regard for the particular instinct to which it may be appealing. Every increase in rate adds directly to the means of self-preservation, of social distinction, and of the accumulation of wealth.

The worker with a fixed salary or wage does not feel as continuously the goad of his wage. It is less in mind and does not control his attitude toward his work. The man on a fixed salary, therefore, will not produce so much.

If he be a workman, he may take better care of his tools, keep his output up to a higher standard of quality, prepare himself for more responsible positions. If he be a salesman, he may be more considerate of his customers and hence really more valuable to his employer; he may be more loyal to the house and hence <p 145> promote the ``team work" of the organization, and he may because of his more receptive state of mind be preparing himself for much greater usefulness to his house. If he be a superintendent, he may be more thoughtful of his men, or more scrupulous for the future of the business.

Production methods or labor conditions are often such that piecework is impossible. There are many functions and processes which thus far have not been satisfactorily adjusted to task systems; there are others (the inspection service in a factory, for instance) where a premium on increased output would defeat the first purpose of the service. Where results can be accurately measured, however, and the quality of the service can be automatically secured or is not sacrificed by concentration upon quantity, the task system—whether it take the form of piece rates, premiums, or bonus—has such superior psychological advantages that it will probably come more and more into use.

Under the general heading quoted above— <p 146>

``How do you make the most of the wages paid your employees?"—the following question was asked: ``What special method do you employ to make men satisfied or pleased with their wages?" The answers were most interesting and instructive. One manager having many thousand men in his organization narrated various methods by which he kept in personal touch with his men, and turned this personal relationship to the advantage of the house.

One illustration will make clear the line he pursued. In the card catalogue of the employees, the birthday of each is noted, the executive recognizing that for the average man this is an anniversary even more important than New Year's.

If for any reason a member of the organization deserves or requires the executive's personal attention, his birthday may be chosen as the date of the interview. Then whether the man merits an advance for extra good work or needs help to correct a temporary slump in efficiency, the reward or the appeal takes on added meaning <p 147> because it coincides with a turning point in his life.

To facilitate the plan, the manager's file of employment cards is arranged, not by initials or departments, but by birthdays. Each workman's name falls under his eye a few days in advance, long enough to secure a report from his foreman, if knowledge is lacking of his progress.

As I entered this manager's office, I met a young man coming out. He had been in the company's employ only a few months and his relations with the organization had not yet been established. Asked for a report, his foreman gave him a good record and recommended a small advance. Imagine the surprise, the instant access of pride and loyalty, the impulse towards greater effort and efficiency, when the young man was called into the manager's office on his birthday, congratulated on his record, and informed that he would start his new year with an advance in wages. Double the advance, if allowed in the usual way, would not have so impressed and satisfied <p 148> him. The increased wage made its appeal direct to the instinct for social recognition, and hence was very effective.

Such a method does not admit of general application. Practiced in cold blood, it might even be harmful. But in this case, it struck me not as an act of selfish cleverness, but as the expression of a real sympathy and interest which the manager felt for his men. The cleverness lay in the recognition that no man is ever so susceptible to counsel, to appreciation, or to rebuke as on his birthday, when the social self is especially alert.

In other organizations, the effort to extend this factor of human sympathy to each worker and to see that full justice is rendered to him takes the form of a department of promotion and discharge. The head is the direct representative of the ``front office'' and is independent of superintendents and foremen. No man can be ``paid off'' until the facts have been submitted to the consideration of this department. Here also the man may present his case to an unprejudiced and sympathetic arbiter. <p 149>

In actual practice the man ``paid off'' is sometimes retained and the foreman, on the evidence of prejudice, bad temper, or other incompetency, is discharged. In consequence every workman knows that his place does not *depend upon the whim of his immediate superior, but that faithful service will certainly be recognized.*

Furthermore, this department assumes the task of shifting men from one department to another and thus minimizing the misfits which lower the efficiency of the whole organization. Records of each man's performance are kept, and promotions and discharge are more nearly in accord with facts than would be possible in a large house without some such agency. In too many big establishments the individual feels that he does not count in the crowd and that he is helpless to do anything to advance himself or to protect himself against an antagonistic foreman. In large measure, such a department reduces this feeling and bridges the chasm between the men and the firm.

In its effect on the attitude and efficiency of employees, the method of fixing and ad- <p 150> justing wages is no less important than the wages themselves. The steady trend of the labor market has been upward and always upward; it is one of the notable achievements of trade and industry that this constant appreciation in the price of man power has been neutralized by increase in the efficiency of its application. This increase in earning capacity has been secured not alone by the development of automatic machinery, but by the division of labor, the subdivision of processes, and the education of workers to accept the new methods, and acquire expert skill in some specialty.

Hardly a generation has passed since one man, or perhaps two working together, built farm wagons, steam engines, and a thousand other articles entire. Now a hundred mechanics or machine tenders may have contributed to either wagon or engine before it reaches the shipping department. Three fourths of these workers are paid piece rates. The substitution of these piece rates for day wages, the striking of a satisfactory balance between production and compensation, and <p 151> the endless changes in the scale as new parts or faster or simpler processes are invented— have all been operations in which the tact and man-handling skill of executives have played a significant part.

In the larger organization this knowledge or skill is often supplied by a manager who has ``come up through the ranks" and has not forgotten his journeyman's dexterity on the way or neglected to keep in touch with improved methods.

Frequently the advantage of a small industry or trading venture over its larger rivals depends on the owner's mastery of all the processes or conditions involved and his ability to deal with his employees on a personal plane in fixing wages or in establishing the standard day's work.

In a stove factory where four fifths of the processes are paid by piece rates, it was necessary, not long ago, to fix the remuneration for the assembling of a new type of range. Most of the operations were standard; the workmen and the management differed, however, on what should be paid for the setting and fas- <p 152> tening of a back piece with seventeen bolts. The men asked fifteen cents a range. When refused, they named twelve cents as an ultimatum. The company was willing neither to pay such a price nor to antagonize the workmen.

The dispute was settled by a demonstration. The superintendent was himself a graduate from the bench and had been an expert workman. The company's contract with the assemblers' union set $4.50 a day as the maximum wage. To prove his contention that even twelve cents was too great a price, he set the back pieces on ten ranges himself, under the eyes of a committee, and proved that at six cents a range he could easily earn the maximum day wage. The price agreed upon was eight cents, little more than half the original demand. Without the demonstration the men would have accepted twelve cents reluctantly.

In the course of the interviews with employers, it became evident that there was agreement on one point—to educate the worker to realize that the house's policy in <p 153> handling its men gave added value to the sums paid out in wages.

The shiftless or unskilled man works mainly for the next pay envelope, with little or no regard for the continuity of employment, the possibility of promotion, of pension, of sick or accident benefits, of working conditions, or the like.

The skilled worker, on the contrary, and the more desirable class of laborers, nearly always rate their wages above or below par, according to the presence or the absence of these contingent benefits or emoluments.

To the average man with a family, the ``steady job" at fair wages is the first consideration. It appeals more strongly to him than intermittent employment at a much higher rate; while the younger, restless, and less dependable man, both skilled and unskilled, gravitates to the shop where he can command a premium for a little while. Just as managers are always looking for the steady worker, nearly all agree in assuring their employees that faithful and efficient service will be rewarded with continuous employment. <p 154>

To carry out this policy is sometimes difficult in businesses where demand is seasonal and where a large part of the product must be made to order. Nevertheless, the manager who adjusts his production program to cover the entire year has the choice of the best workers even when other factories offer higher rates. Likewise, the employer who sacrifices his profit in bad years to ``take care of his men" and hold his organization together recovers his losses when the revival comes.

So deeply rooted is this desire for a ``steady job" and so generally recognized as an essential of the labor problem that several large industries have developed ``side lines" to which they can turn their organization during their slack seasons; while others in periods of depression pile up huge stocks of standard products, making heavy investments of capital, for the primary purpose of keeping their men employed.

How such a policy reacts on the wage question, and hence on the efficiency of employees, is shown by an instance which lately fell under <p 155> my notice. By a long and persistent campaign of education and demonstration, a small ``quality" house forced a rival ten times as large to adopt the careful processes on which this quality depended. Adopting the small man's methods, the competitor, instead of training its own operatives to the new standards, sought to hire the other man's skilled workers. The premium offered was a thirty per cent advance. It was refused, however. The tempted mechanics, analyzing the rival's proposal, hit on the disloyalty contemplated towards its own employees. They were to be discharged or transferred to other departments to make room for the new men.

Measuring this cold-blooded policy against the consideration, the unfailing effort of their old employer to ``take care of them" in bad seasons, the workers decided to stick to the smaller company and refuse the advance.

Next to continuous employment, among methods of increasing the value of wages, is the policy of making promotions from the ranks.

This practice seems to be commonly ac- <p 156> cepted as fruitful, although many firms believe it impossible of application in filling some of the higher as well as some of the more technical positions. Where the system is applicable, it acts as a powerful stimulus to the men by adding to their present wages the promise or possibility of better positions and higher pay in the future. It gives assurance of promotion for faithful service much greater than in houses which fill the upper positions from outside sources on the assumption that they thus get ``new blood'' into the business. The men secured from outside may be more skilled or more productive of immediate results than any available in the house organization. By their importation, however, the wages of all the men aspiring to the position have been cheapened. Nor does the evil stop there.

The assumption is naturally drawn that the same practice is likely to be followed in filling other vacancies. The stimulus to initiative and activity is thus weakened for men in every grade and their wages are shrunk below par. <p 157>

The importance which some successful employers attach to this principle of promotion from the ranks is well illustrated by an incident which recently occurred in a large manufacturing establishment organized on a one-man basis. During the president's absence it was decided to open up a new zone of trade for a new product. No one in the organization knew the product and the field, so a new man was put in charge. The work progressed surprisingly well; the enterprise was in every way successful.

When the real head returned, he called his managers together and told them that the new man must be removed and the most deserving man in the regular organization appointed in his place. He was met with the protest that no employee was capable of taking up the work and reminded that the new man had already achieved great success. The president answered that he was willing to lose money in the department for the first year rather than cheapen and disorganize the service by taking away the certainty of promotion and by re- <p 158> moving the incentive to study and self-development which had increased the efficiency of every ambitious employee.

Innumerable examples of the same principle in promotions could be gleaned from the records of some of the oldest and most progressive houses in the country. In one establishment visited, the quality of whose wares is strenuously guarded, it was discovered that the chemist and metallurgist in charge of the factory laboratory had been lifted out of one of the departments and supplied with the money to take a specialized course in physics, chemistry, and metallurgy. The advertising manager, the factory engineer, and two or three of the foremen had been given leaves of absence to study and fit themselves for the positions to which their talents and inclinations drew them. Even among the workmen there was a fixed basis for advancement towards the better jobs and the higher rates, dependent on satisfactory service and output.

To these major considerations in increasing the worth of wages, those companies which <p 159> have given the longest attention to the problem add many other inducements.

An efficient and contented employee has a positive money value to any employer. To hold him and keep him efficient, his personal comfort and needs should be considered in every way not detrimental to the company's interests.

As nearly as possible, the ideal in factory location and construction is approached. Some industries have removed bodily to country towns, less for the sake of a cheap site than for the purpose of establishing themselves where housing conditions for workers were good, rents low, the cost of living cheaper, and other factors tending to *add value* to every dollar paid in wages were present. Direct appeal was made to the intelligence of employees, whose health is part of their capital, by making and keeping working conditions as healthful and sanitary, as little taxing on eyesight and bodily vigor as circumstances and judicious investment of capital allowed. Scores of towns have been built outright, to benefit employees. <p 160>

In line with this policy are the systems of benefit insurance for accident and sickness maintained and partly supported by many companies; the pension systems which have been adopted within the last few years by some of the greatest and most progressive companies in America; the free medical service, both in case of factory accidents and sickness at home, which other firms provide for employees; and various other activities contributing to the welfare of workers, both during working hours and afterwards.

Employers are coming more and more to see that this is the case and to devote both thought and money to the elimination of conditions which cut wages below par.

Whatever reduces hazard, discomfort, loss of time, uncertainty, or the cost of living for workers adds value to their wages and is a means of influencing their attitude towards the company.

Some employers are continually exercised to keep the wages of their men from falling below par. Others are equally solicitous that their men may regard their wages as above <p 161> par. This classification is a real one and was made plain by some of the interviews referred to above. Thus in answer to the question, ``What special method do you employ to make men satisfied or pleased with their wages?" one employer immediately put his own interpretation on the question. To him it meant, ``What method do you employ to keep your men from being *dissatisfied with their wages?"

His answer was: ``By paying them somewhere near what they ask or expect. If we don't," he added, ``they go out on strike and we have to compromise."

The majority of successful employers have advanced beyond this negative, defensive attitude and take a positive and aggressive position in dealing with the problem.

Instead of assuming their work accomplished when the men are not dissatisfied or rebellious, they do not rest until every dollar paid out in wages is above par in its influence upon efficiency.

Thus in innumerable ways the progressive employer increases the value of all wages he <p 162> pays by making them appeal to the reason and to the instincts of workers in a way un- dreamed of by less enlightened men. The purpose of wages is to produce a certain psychological effect and to promote the most favorable attitude on the part of the worker. The methods of increasing the purchasing power of money thus spent is one of the most interesting and yet complex problems which the business man has to face.

This chapter shows the psychological ground for the following statements:—

Employees differ in their response to piecework rates and to salaries. Some respond more satisfactorily to one and some to the other.

When the development of men for better positions is of prime importance, the piecework system is not to be adopted. If the quantity of work per unit of wage is of greatest importance, then some form of wage other than fixed salary should be used.

An employee should not be dismissed as hopelessly lazy till he has shown this attitude <p 163> in more than one department or has failed to respond to different forms of stimulation.

Changes in wages may often be placed under the authority of some person or committee other than the immediate superiors of the employees involved. This authority may be vested in the direct representatives of the executives or in such a committee as would be formed by representatives of the executives and also employees from the different departments of the establishment.

Payment of wages, so far as possible, should be made to appeal to the instincts for social distinction and for acquisition as well as to the instinct for self-preservation.

Wages should never be reduced without a tactful and sincere attempt to convince the men of the necessity of such an act.

Increase in wages may well be made a personal matter. Some firms, however, are most successful with a mechanical wage system in which employees know exactly the conditions necessary for an increase in wages.

All work should be thoroughly supervised <p 164> and inspected so that employees know that good service will be recognized and rewarded.

The policy of filling all positions from the ranks seems growing in favor, since it gives certain hope for advancement and hence greater satisfaction with the present wage.

The wage may well include a tacit insurance for the future. Employees should be assured that so long as they remain faithful to the firm, their work and pay will continue, and that in accident or old age they will be provided for. Accepted thus, the wage secures increased service.

CHAPTER VII

PLEASURE

AS A MEANS OF INCREASING HUMAN EFFICIENCY

TO prevent the usual ``summer slump" in output, the manager of a factory employing a hundred or more sewing girls on piecework tried various methods. He began with closer individual supervision by the forewomen. He set up a bulletin board and posted daily the names of the five highest operators. He added small cash prizes weekly. He adopted a modified bonus system framed so as not to interfere with the established average of winter tasks. With each his success was only partial. Ten or a dozen of the more energetic girls responded to the stimulus; on the majority the effect was slight.

The problem was serious. June, July, and August comprised the season when his prod- <p 165> <p 166> ucts were at a premium, when future orders were frequently lost because partial deliveries could not be made immediately. Studying the question, he noted specifically, what he already knew, that the output dropped as the temperature rose. A cool day sandwiched into a week of hot weather frequently equaled the best winter records. This fact, coupled with the observation that the spirit of his working force seemed to change with the change of temperature from warm to cold, helped him to arrive at the right solution.

He made the discovery sitting in the draught of an electric fan. He looked up, made a mental note; and next morning he moved his office ``comforter" out to the head of one file of machines. The draught tangled the goods under the seamstresses' hands at times, but the half dozen girls within range showed a decided increase in production over the day before and over operators at other tables.

He had found his remedy for the summer slump. Within a week he had installed a system of large overhead fans and an exhaust <p 167> blower and saw his production figures mount to the winter's best average. From careless, indifferent workers, on edge at trifles and difficult to hold, his force developed steadiness and efficiency. Not only was the output increased twenty per cent over previous summers, but the proportion of spoiled work was considerably reduced.

One of the women who had been a subject of the first day's experiment struck close to the reason of her greater efficiency in her off-hand answer to his inquiry.

``It was a pleasure to work to-day. It was so comfortable after yesterday you just forgot the other girls, forgot you wanted to rest, forgot everything but the seams you were running and the fact that it was a big day. I'm not near so tired as usual either."

A successful day is likely to be a restful one, an unsuccessful day an exhausting one. The man who is greatly interested in his work and who finds delight in overcoming the difficulties of his calling is not likely to become so tired as the man for whom the work is a burden. <p 168>

The experience related summarizes the experience of every worker who has studied, either on his own initiative or at some other's instance, the effect upon output secured by the removal of distressing or displeasing conditions from the workroom.

The man who has been engaged in intellectual or manual labor finds himself more or less exhausted when the day's work is done. The degree of exhaustion varies greatly from day to day and is not in direct proportion to the amount of energy expended or the results attained. A comparatively busy day may leave him feeling fresh, while at the end of a day much less occupied he may be utterly ``dragged out'' and weary.

Some men habitually find themselves fatigued, while others ordinarily end the day with a feeling of vigor. These contrary effects are not necessarily due primarily to disparity in the amount of energy spent or to unequal stores of energy available. The discrepancy in many instances is due to diverse attitudes toward the work or varying <p 169> degrees of success which has attended the work.

Pleasure secured in and from work is the best preventive and balm for tired muscles and jaded brains. Dislike or discomfort, on the other hand, adds to toil by sapping the strength of the worker.

Victory in intercollegiate athletic events depends on will power and physical endurance. This is particularly apparent in football. Frequently it is not the team with the greater muscular development or speed of foot that wins the victory, but the one with the more grit and perseverance. At the conclusion of a game players are often unable to walk from the field and need to be carried. Occasionally the winning team has actually worked the harder and received the more serious injuries. Regardless of this fact, it is usually true that the victorious team leaves the field less jaded than the conquered team. Furthermore the winners will report next day refreshed and ready for further training, while the losers may require several days to <p 170> overcome the shock and exhaustion of their defeat.

Recently I had a very hard contest at tennis. Some hours after the game I was still too tired to do effective work. I wondered why, until I remembered that I had been thoroughly beaten, and that, too, by an opponent whom I felt I outclassed. I had been in the habit of playing even harder contests and ordinarily with no discomfort—especially when successful in winning the match.

What I have found so apparent in physical exertion is equally true in intellectual labor. Writing or research work which progresses satisfactorily leaves me relatively fresh; unsuccessful efforts bring their aftermath of weariness.

Intellectual work which is pleasant is stimulating and does not fag one, while intellectual work which is uninteresting or displeasing is depressing and exhausting.

We can readily trace the source of energy in mechanical devices. The hands of a clock continue in their course because of the energy <p 171> locked up in a compressed spring or elevated weight. The gun projects the bullet because of the sudden chemical union of carbon with saltpeter and sulphur. The steam engine takes its energy from the steam secured by combustion of coal or other fuel.

The work of the human organism is usually classified as muscular or intellectual. In either the expenditure of energy is as dependent upon known causes as is the activity of the mechanical devices mentioned above.

Every muscular activity is dependent upon muscular cells ready for combustion; without such combustion no muscular work is performed.

Every intellectual process is likewise dependent upon brain cells ready for combustion, and no intellectual work can be performed without combustion of these brain cells.

To secure continued activity the clock must be rewound, the gun must be recharged, more coal must be supplied to the engine. In like manner the continuation of muscular and in- <p 172> tellectual activity depends upon the restoration of muscle and brain cells. The necessity for renewal is greater or less according to the amount stored in reserve and the rapidity of consumption. A maximum head of steam may keep the engine running for a long time unless the load is too heavy or the speed too great. Though under certain conditions the amount of muscle and brain energy stored in reserve is large, continuous or rapid activity of necessity expends the reserve and leads to exhaustion.

It is a simple process to rewind the clock, to reload the gun, and to replenish the fuel. To restore muscular and nerve cells is a very delicate process. So wonderful is the human organism, however, that the process is carried on perfectly without our consciousness or volition except under abnormal conditions.

Food and air are the first essentials of this restoration. Indirectly the perfect working of all the bodily organs contribute to the process — especially deepened breathing, heightened pulse, and increase of bodily volume due <p 173> to the expansion of the blood vessels running just beneath the skin.

Here pleasure enters. Its effect on the expenditure of energy is to make muscle and brain cells more available for consumption, and particularly to hasten the process of restoration or recuperation.

The deepened breathing supplies more air for the oxidation of body wastes. The heightened pulse carries nourishment more rapidly to the depleted tissues and relieves the tissues more rapidly from the poisonous wastes produced by work. The body, the machine, runs more smoothly, and fewer stops for repairs are made necessary.

In addition to these specific functions, pleasure hastens all the bodily processes which are of advantage to the organism. The hastening may be so great that recuperation keeps pace with the consumption consequent on efficient labor, with the result that there is little or no exhaustion. This is in physiological terms the reason why a person can do more when he ``enjoys'' his work or play, and can <p 174> continue his efforts for a longer period without fatigue. The man who enjoys his work requires less time for recreation and exercise, for his enjoyment recharges the storage battery of energy.

Not only can I endure more and achieve more when I take pleasure in the task, but I can also secure better results from others by providing for their interest and for their pleasure in what they are doing. This is a fact which wise merchants and employers have felt intuitively, but in most instances the principle has not been consciously formulated. High-grade stores do much to add to the pleasure of their customers. Every resource of art and architecture is employed to make store rooms appeal to the <ae>sthetic sense and the appreciation of customers. Clerks are instructed to be obliging and courteous. Employees are not allowed to dress in a style likely to offend a customer and they are schooled in manners and in speech. Space is devoted to the convenience and comfort of customers. <p 175>

The most successful establishments in the world are the ones which do most to please their patrons—not by cutting prices or simply by supplying better goods, but by expediting and making more pleasant the purchase of goods.

They have discovered that customers inducted into a beautiful shop and surrounded by tactful obliging clerks are more willing to buy and are more likely to be satisfied with what they purchase. By adding to their patrons' comfort and pleasure they are able to accomplish more than by any other selling argument. In like manner, restaurants and hotels have learned that splendid rooms, flowers, spotless linen, well-dressed and courteous waiters, good furniture, and so on, all attract customers and induce them to order more generously.

Lawyers find in trying cases that it is quite essential to regard the mood of clients, juries, and judges. The pleased man is not suspicious; he does not hesitate in coming to a conclusion, and he is not likely to impute evil motives to the actions of others. As has been <p 176> well said by Dickens, when speaking from the viewpoint of the defendant, ``A good, contented, well-breakfasted juryman is a capital thing to get hold of. Discontented or hungry jurymen always find for the plaintiff."

The salesman with a pleasing personality is able to sell more goods than others less happily endowed. Some salesmen try to supplement this power —or supply the lack of a pleasing personality—by ``jollying" the possible customer in various ways. Dinners, theaters, cigars, and various other devices are thus used, and in many instances with success.

Modern business employs such methods less and less, chiefly because the customer recognizes the purpose of the attempt, and either refuses to accept the ``hospitality" or is on his guard to resist the effect. A pleasing personality, however, inspires confidence, tends to put the customer in a good humor and optimistic mood, and results in sales.

A cold, formal manner, ill temper, or a pessimistic outlook, on the contrary, will <p 177> handicap the sale of the best merchandise made.

A man is said to be suggestible when he comes to conclusions or acts without due deliberation. Suggestion, then, is nothing but the mental condition which causes us to believe and respond without the normal amount of weighing of evidence. While in a suggestible condition we are credulous, responsive, and impulsive. Such a mental condition is favored and induced by pleasure. Discomfort or dissatisfaction with the conditions or surroundings prompts the opposing attitude; we become suspicious and slow to act or believe. While in a suggestible condition, we place our orders freely and promptly. The merchant who can please his customers and bring them to a suggestible mood before he displays his wares, therefore, has done much to secure generous sales.

Advantageous results from suggestion are not limited to the relationship between buyer and seller.

The pleased and satisfied employee is open <p 178> to the suggestions of foreman and manager and responds with an enthusiasm impossible of generation in one dissatisfied from any cause.

Methods of insuring this pleasure in work for employees are yet in the formative stage. Until recently the want of such methods, indeed, was not felt. The slave driver with the most profane vocabulary and the greatest recklessness in the use of fist and foot was supposed to be the most effective type of boss. The task system set an irreducible minimum for the day's work; the employer exacted the task and assumed that no better way of handling men could be devised. Piecework rates provided a better and more reasonable basis for securing something like a maximum day's work; bonus and premium systems have carried the incentive of the wage in increasing efficiency to the last point short of co<o:>perative organization. But all of these systems fall short in assuming that men are machines; that their powers and capacities are fixed quantities; that the efficiency of a well-disposed and industrious employee ought to be proof against <p 179> varying conditions or environment; that a man can achieve the desired standard, if only he has the will to achieve it.

Discipline has become less brutal if not less strict. The laborer works, not alone to avoid poverty and hunger, but to secure the means of pleasure.

It is not so long since harsh discipline was common both in homes and in business. The boy worked hard because he was afraid not to. The man labored because poverty threatened him if idle. We were in what might be called a ``pain economy''; we worked to escape pain. To-day this has largely been changed.

Employers, too, are experimenting boldly with the idea of creating pleasure in work. The first step has been taken in the very general elimination of the old wasteful, neglectful elements of factory and office environment. Comfort, the first neutral element of pleasure, is provided for employees just as solid foundations are provided for the factory buildings. There is light, heat, and ventilation where a generation ago there were tiny windows, <p 180> shadows, lonely stoves, and foul air. Cleanliness is provided and preserved; not a few of the larger industries employ a regular corps of janitors to keep floors, walls, and windows clean. The walls are tinted; the lights are arranged so as to provide the right illumination without straining the workers' eyes. The departments are symmetrically arranged; the aisles are wide; the working space is ample; there is no fear to haunt machine tenders that a mis- step or a moment of forgetfulness will entangle them in a neighboring machine. The factory buildings themselves, without being pretentious, have pleasing, simple lines and unobtrusive ornamentation. They look like, and are, when the human equation does not interfere, *pleasant places to work in.

This is the typical modern factory; thousands can be found in America. On this foundation of good working conditions and pleasant environment, many companies have built more or less elaborate systems of welfare work, whose effectiveness in creating pleasure and efficiency seem to depend on the <p 181> purpose and spirit of the men behind them. These systems frequently begin with beautification of the factory premises and workrooms —window boxes, factory lawns, ivied walls, trees, and shrubs—and advance by various stages to lunch rooms for workers, factory libraries, rest rooms for women workers, factory nurses and physicians, and sometimes the development of a social life among employees through picnics, lectures, dances, night schools, and like activities. The methods employed are too diverse and too recent to permit an accurate estimate of their work or a true analysis of the elements of their success. It is incumbent on the employer to find or work out for himself the method best suited to his individual needs.

To understand how pleasure heightens the suggestibility of the individual it is but necessary to consider the well-known effects which pleasure has on the various bodily and mental processes.

The action of pleasure and displeasure upon the muscles of the body is most apparent. With displeasure the muscles of the forehead <p 182> contract; folds and wrinkles appear. The corners of the mouth are drawn down; the head bowed; the shoulders stoop and draw together over the breast; the chest is contracted; the fingers of the hand close, and there is also a tendency to bend the arms so as to protect the fore part of the body. In displeasure the body is thus seen to contract and to put itself on the defensive. It closes itself to outside influences and attempts to ``withdraw within its shell."

With pleasure the forehead is smoothed out; the corners of the mouth are lifted; the head is held erect; the shoulders are thrown back; the chest is expanded; the fingers of the hand are opened, and the arm is ready to go out to grasp any object. The whole body is thrown into a receptive attitude. It is prepared to be affected by outside stimulations and is ready to profit by them.

That these characteristic bodily attitudes of pleasure and displeasure have an effect on the mind is evident. Bodily and mental attitudes have developed together in the history <p 183> of the race. The conditions which cause a receptive attitude of body cause also a suggestible state of mind. The conditions which call for bodily protection also demand a suspicious and non-responsive attitude of mind. The bodily and the mental attitudes have become so intimately associated that the presence of one assures the presence of the other.

Pleasure and a particular attitude of body are indissolubly united, and when these two are present, a suggestible condition of mind seems of necessity to follow.

Thus by the subtle working of pleasant impressions the customer is disarmed of his suspicion and made ready to respond to the suggestions of the merchant.

The effect of the suggestible attitude of the body, as produced by pleasure, is increased by certain other effects which pleasure produces on the body.

Muscular strength is frequently measured by finding the maximum grip on a recording instrument. The amount of the grip varies from time to time and is affected by various <p 184> conditions. One of the phenomena which has been thoroughly investigated is the effect of pleasure and of pain on the intensity of the grip. It is well established that pleasure increases the grip or the available amount of energy. Displeasure reduces the strength.

The total volume of the body would seem to be constant for any particular short interval of time. Such, however, is not the case.

With pleasure the lungs are filled with air from deepened breathing; the volume of the limbs is increased by the increased flow of blood. Pleasure thus actually makes us larger and displeasure smaller.

This increase in muscular strength and bodily volume due to pleasure has a very decided effect upon the mind. The increase of muscular strength gives us a feeling of power and assurance, the increase in volume gives us a feeling of expansion and importance. These conditions produced by increase of muscular strength and bodily volume contribute to the general suggestible condition described above.

If I am in a suggestible condition and if I <p 185> also feel an unusual degree of assurance in my own powers and importance, I shall have such confidence in the wisdom of my intended acts that there will seem to be no ground for delay. Furthermore the increased action of the heart, due to the effect of pleasure, gives me a feeling of buoyancy and invigoration which adds appreciably to the tendency to action.

We thus see why pleasure renders us more suggestible and hence makes us more apt to purchase proffered merchandise or to respond to the suggestions of our foreman or our executive. We also see why it is that a man may increase his efficiency by pleasing those with whom he has to work, whether they be customers or employees.

CHAPTER VIII

THE LOVE OF THE GAME

AS A MEANS OF INCREASING HUMAN EFFICIENCY

THE motives discussed in previous chapters are fairly adequate for developing efficiency in all except the owner or chief executive. The employee may imitate and compete with his equals and his superiors; he may work for his wage, and he may be loyal to the house. To increase the industry and enthusiasm of the head is a task of supreme importance. Interest and enthusiasm must be kindled at the top that the spark may be passed down to the lower levels. It can never travel in the opposite direction.

How, then, is the president to light his fires and transmit his enthusiasm to his managers and other subordinates? Not by working for <p 186> <p 187> money alone, nor through imitation, competition, or loyalty to the works of his own hands. All these may be essential, may be powerful subordinate incentives to action, but singly or collectively they are not adequate. In any organization, the head who attains the maximum of success must depend for his enthusiasm upon an instinctive love of the game.

The subordinate possessing such love of the game and independent of others for his enthusiasm is sure to rise. The subject is, therefore, of vital importance both to the executive and to the ambitious employee. Every employer feels the need of such an attitude towards work, both in himself and in his men.

An attempt will be made in this chapter to comprehend this instinctive love of the game, to discuss to what extent it is inherited and to what extent subject to cultivation, and to analyze the conditions most favorable for its development in respect to one's own work as well as that of his employees.

The love of the game is in part instinctive, <p 188> and its nature is made clear by consideration of certain of the instincts of animals.

The young lion spends much time in pretended stalking of game and in harmless struggles with his mates. He takes great delight in the exercise of his cunning and in his strength of limb and jaw. Fortunately for the young lion this is the sort of activity best adapted to develop his strength of muscle and his cunning in capturing prey. However, it is not for the sake of the training that the young lion performs these particular acts. He does them simply because he loves to. In like manner the young greyhound chasing his mates and the young squirrel gathering and storing nuts have no thought beyond the instinctive pleasure they find in performing these functions. To each there is no other form of activity so satisfactory.

Man possesses more instincts than any of the lower animals. One pronounced instinct in all normal males is the hunting instinct. Grover Cleveland went fishing because he loved the sport, not because of the value of <p 189> the fish caught. Theodore Roosevelt did not hunt big game in Africa because he was in need of luscious steaks or tawny hides. He was not working solely in the interest of the Smithsonian Institute nor to secure material for his book. Doubtless these were subsidiary motives, but the chief reason why he killed the game was that he instinctively loves the sport. He endured the hardships of Africa for the same reason that fishermen spend days in the icy water of a trout stream and hunters lie still for hours suffering intense cold for a chance to shoot at a bear.

For some men, buying and selling is as great a delight as felling a deer. For others the manufacture of goods is as great a joy as landing a trout. For such a man enthusiasm for his work is unfailing and industry unremittent.

He is suited to his task as is the cub to the fight, the puppy to the chase, the squirrel to the burying of nuts, or the hunter to the killing of game. His labor always appeals to him as the thing of supremest moment. His interest in it is such that it never fails to in- <p 190> spire others by contagion. For such a man laziness or indifference in business seems anomalous, while industry and enthusiasm are as natural as the air he breathes and as inexhaustible as the air itself.

By classifying the love of the game as an instinct, we seem to admit that it is born and not developed; that some men possess it and others do not; that if a man possesses it, he does not need to cultivate it, and that if he does not possess, he cannot acquire it. There is doubtless much truth in this, but fortunately it is not the whole truth.

Some instincts are specific—even stereotyped —and not subject to cultivation or change. Thus the bee's instinctive method of gathering and storing honey is very specific and definite. The bee is unable to modify its routine to any great extent. The bee which does not instinctively perform the different acts properly will never learn to.

There are other instincts not so stereotyped in manner or constant in degree. The instincts of man are much more variable than <p 191> those of the lower animals and are much more subject to direction, inhibition, or development. If this love of the game were solely a matter of inheritance, if the business genius were born and not made, and if it could not be cultivated and developed, our hope for the improvement of the race would be small.

Potential geniuses exist in large numbers but fail of discovery because they are not developed. Instincts manifest themselves only in the presence of certain stimulating conditions. They are developed by exercise and stimulated further by the success attending upon their exercise.

Thus certain conditions, more or less definite, are effective in determining the line along which instincts shall manifest themselves, and the extent to which the instincts shall be developed and then ultimately supplemented by experience and reason.

Fortunately we have reason to believe that although the business genius must have a good inheritance, yet the inheritance does not determine what its possessor shall make of himself. <p 192> Many persons are inclined to overestimate the influence of inheritance in determining success in business. The folly of this attitude is every day becoming more and more apparent.

The conditions essential for developing the love of the game in business may be summarized under three heads:—

First, a man will develop a love of the game in any business in which he is led to assume a responsibility, to take personal initiative, to feel that he is creating something, and that he is expressing himself in his work.

As organizations become larger and more complex in their methods, there is a corresponding increase in the difficulty of making the employees retain and develop this feeling of independent and creative responsibility. Business has become so specialized and the work of the individual seems so petty that he is not likely to feel that he is expressing himself through his work or to retain a feeling of independence. Properly conceived, there is no position in trade or industry which does not warrant such <p 193> an attitude. To promote this attitude various devices have been adopted by business firms. Some try to put a real responsibility on each employee and to make him feel it. Others have devised forms of partnership which give numerous employees shares in the business and so help to develop this attitude.

In developing men for responsible positions this attitude must be secured and retained even while they are occupying the lesser positions.

Few things so stimulate a boy as the feeling that he is responsible for a certain task, that he is expressing himself in it, that he is creating something worth while.

Many managers and more foremen are unable to develop this feeling in their subordinates because they assume all the responsibility and allow those under them no share of it. On the other hand, some executives have the happy faculty of inspiring this attitude in all their men. The late Marshall Field made partners of his lieutenants and encouraged them to assume responsibility and to do <p 194> creative work. As a result they developed a love of the game—a fact to which he owed much of his phenomenal success.

The second condition or factor in the development of the love of the game in business is social prestige.

We have but partially expressed the nature of man when we have spoken of him as delighting in independent self-expression, as being self-centered and self-seeking. Man is inherently social in his nature and desires nothing more than the approval of his fellows. That which society approves we do with enthusiasm. We change our forms of amusements, our manner of life, and our daily occupations according to the whims of society. Fifteen years ago the riding of bicycles was quite the proper thing, and we all trained down till we could ride a century. To-day we are equally enthusiastic in lowering bogy on the golf course. This change in our ambitions is not because it is inherently more fun to beat bogy than to ride a century. The change has come about simply because of the change of <p 195> social prestige secured from the two forms of amusement.

We may expect to find enthusiastic industry in the accomplishment of any task which society looks upon as particularly worthy. During the past few decades in America society has given the capitalist unusual honor and has allowed him monetary rewards unprecedented in the history of the world.

If the capitalist had been honored less than the poet, the preacher, or the soldier, and his material rewards fallen below theirs, our money captains would have been fewer in number.

In spite of occasional muck rakings, society's esteem for the capitalist has been unbounded. He is in general the only man with a national reputation. Society bestows upon him unstinted praise and the most generous rewards for his toil. His rewards are so extravagant that the game seems worthy of every effort he can put forth. Love of the game has consequently been engendered within him, and his enthusiasm has been unbounded. <p 196>

This motive of social prestige is less easy of application to the humbler ranks of employees.

Most men engaged in the industries are entirely deprived of the stimulus because their social group does not look with approval upon their daily tasks. It may even despise men for doing well work essential as preparatory to better positions. There are many young men engaged in perfectly worthy employment who prefer that their social set should not know of the exact nature of their work for fear it would be regarded as menial and not sufficiently ``swell."

This disrespect for honest toil is due to various causes. One cause is that nearly all young men—and indeed most older men too—look upon their present positions merely as stepping stones. They look forward to promotion and more interesting work. They and their social group fail to accord dignity to the work which they are doing at any time.

Another reason why the motive of social prestige has no effect in the more humble <p 197> positions is that in business we have practically abandoned the standard of the artist and adopted that of the capitalist. The artist's standard is diametrically opposed to the capitalistic standard. We honor the capitalist not for what he does, but for the money he gets for what he does. We honor the artist for what he does and never because of the monetary considerations which follow his creation.

To substitute the standard of the artist for the standard of the capitalist would be impossible in business, yet a harmonious working of the two is possible.

Such a harmony was probably present in the old industrial guilds, which developed a class consciousness creating its own ideals. Within the guild the most skillful workman had the highest honor. The work itself, independent of the money which might be received for it, was uppermost in the worker's mind.

The executive seeking to stimulate love of the game among his workmen should in some way see that social approval attaches itself <p 198> to the work as such and not to the wage which is secured by means of the work. The workmen must be given an interest in the work as well as in the wage.

Executives everywhere find that ``getting together" with others engaged in the same work is most stimulating. We are inspired by the presence of others engaged in the same sort of work and giving approval to success in our particular field.

The third condition for securing a love of the game is that the work itself must appeal to the individual as something important and useful.

Its useful function must be apparent, and the necessity and advantage of perfect performance must be emphasized. I play golf because the game permits me to assert myself and engage in independent and exhilarating activity. My devotion to my professional tasks, however, is dependent upon the fact that I regard psychology, whether the work be in research or instruction, as of the greatest importance to science and to mankind in general. The work as a whole and all the <p 199> details of it seem to me to be important. In performing my daily tasks they seem to me to be worthy of the most persistent and enthusiastic effort.

Doubtless there are classes of work incapable of appealing to individuals as does my work to me. But in many instances work seems menial and ignoble because it is not understood. It is not seen in its relationships and broader aspects. The single task as performed by the individual is so small and so specialized that it does not seem worth while.

The dignity of labor demands that the workman should respect the work of his hands.

He should look upon his accomplished tasks as of inherent dignity independent of the monetary recompense to be received. To keep the workman's efficiency keyed up, the employer should see to it that this broader aspect of labor is emphasized and that the day laborer finds some reason for his labor besides his wage. It is the only game he may ever have time to play. It is to the interest of <p 200> himself, his employer, and society at large that he should enter enthusiastically into it and be ennobled by it.

Professional, technical, and vocational schools are serving a noble function in emphasizing the dignity of the work for which they are preparing young men.

They are more and more presenting the broader aspects of the subjects taught. Even the altruistic and extremely technical aspects of the subject are found profitable. The narrower and apparently the more practical course does not result so successfully as the broader and more cultural ones.

The boy who goes direct into work from the public school is not likely to c<o:>ordinate his task with the general activity of the establishment, and he is not likely to see how he is in anyway contributing to the welfare of humanity by his work. He needs to be shown how each line of industry and profession serves a great function, has an interesting history, and is vitally connected with many of the most important human interests. He should learn <p 201> to see how the different cogs are essential and worthy factors in the total process. The boy who thus comprehends his task looks upon it and is inspired by it in a way that would otherwise be quite impossible.

Some of the most successful houses have been so impressed with the importance of this form of industrial education that at their own expense they have established night schools for new employees as well as for those who have been years with the firm. Not only are the students taught how to perform their respective tasks, but a broader program is attempted. Sometimes an attempt is made to lead the students to appreciate the dignity of the particular activity in which the firm is engaged. The history of the firm is then fully presented so that the employees will comprehend the part the house has actually taken in the world. Some firms try to show each man how his work is related to the work of the house as a whole and to other departments. In various ways schools and individual firms are successfully attempting to inject a nobler regard <p 202> and appreciation for labor. The result is most gratifying and manifests itself in increased enthusiasm and other expressions of the increased love of the game.

The three conditions which we have been considering for developing the love of the game are quite different, appeal to the different sides of the individual, and are not all equally applicable to the young man who seeks to become a leader among his fellows or to the manager of men who seeks to develop leaders.

The attitude of independent, creative responsibility appeals to our individualistic and self-centered self. It is an attitude that may be assumed by the ambitious young man and encouraged by the manager. It is absolutely indispensable for developing this much-coveted love of the game in any form of useful endeavor. It is readily assumed or developed in the chief executive, but may be developed in subordinates with great difficulty.

Social prestige appeals to our selfishly social natures, and yet the desire to secure this <p 203> social favor is in the main ennobling. It is of special value to the manager of large groups of men. The manager may create the social atmosphere which is most favorable to the development of the love of the game in his particular industry.

The last condition discussed, regard for the work as important and as useful, makes its appeal to our nobler and what we might in some instances speak of as our altruistic selves. This condition is equally serviceable to the ambitious youth and to the successful superintendent of men. We all look out for number one, but appeals made to the higher self are not unavailing. We are most profoundly stirred when we are appealed to from all sides. However, the love of the game will never be universal in the professional and industrial world. We can scarcely imagine the millennium when all employees would cease to despise their toil and cease to serve for pay alone.

CHAPTER IX

RELAXATION

AS A MEANS OF INCREASING HUMAN EFFICIENCY

Be not therefore anxious for the Morrow

A STUDY of the lives of great men is both interesting and profitable. In such a study we are amazed at the records of the deeds of the men whom the world calls great. The results of the labors of Hercules seem to be approximated according to many of these truthful accounts.

In studying the lives of contemporary business men two facts stand out prominently. The first is that their labors have brought about results that to most of us would have seemed impossible. Such men appear as giants, in comparison with whom ordinary men sink to the size of pygmies.

The second fact which a study of successful <p 204> <p 205> business men (or any class of successful men) reveals is that they never seem rushed for time.

Men noted for efficiency almost never appear to be hurried. They have plenty of time to accomplish their tasks, and therefore can afford to take their work leisurely.

Such men have time to devote to objects in no way connected with their business. It cannot be regarded as accidental that this characteristic of mind is found so commonly among successful men during the years of their most fruitful labor.

According to the American Ideal, the man who is sure to succeed is one who is continuously ``keyed up to concert pitch," who is ever alert and is always giving attention to his business or profession. As far as the captains of industry are concerned, such is not the case. They devote relatively few hours a day to their strenuous toil, but they keep a cool head and a steady hand. They are always composed, never confused, but ever ready to attack a new problem with their maximum ability. They <p 206> follow the injunction of Christ expressed in His Sermon on the Mount: ``Be not therefore anxious for the morrow."

Of all the nations of the world, Americans are supposed to be the hardest working. We have attributed our industrial success to the fact that there is a bustle and snap to our work which are not equaled in any other country. But recent students of the industrial world are now telling us that even in the case of day and piece labor this characteristic is frequently a weakness rather than an advantage. They say that the American product ``suffers from hurry, want of finish, and want of solidity."— ``Industrial Efficiency," Arthur Shadwell, Vol. 1, p. 26.

In the great middle class of American society, there is a lack of repose and an absence of relaxation which astonishes foreign observers.

They tell us that we are wild-eyed and too intense. Dr. Clauston of Scotland is quoted as saying:—

``You Americans wear too much expression in your faces. You are living like an army <p 207> with all its reserves engaged in action. The duller countenance of the British population betokens a better scheme of life. They suggest stores of reserved nervous force to fall back upon, if any occasion should arise that requires it. The inexcitability, this presence at all times of power not used, I regard as the great safeguard of our British people. The other thing in you gives me a sense of insecurity, and you ought somehow to tone yourselves down. You do really carry too much expression, you take too intensely the trivial moments of life."

The late Professor William James of Harvard makes the following pertinent remark concerning the overtension of Americans:—

``Your intense, convulsive worker breaks down and has bad moods so often that you never know where he may be when you most need his help, —he may be having one of his `bad days.' We say that so many of our fellow-countrymen collapse, and have to be sent abroad to rest their nerves, because they work so hard. I suspect that this is an im- <p 208> mense mistake. I suspect that neither the nature nor the amount of our work is accountable for the frequency and severity of our breakdowns, but that their cause lies rather in those absurd feelings of hurry and having no time, in that breathlessness and tension, that anxiety of feature and that solicitude of results, that lack of inner harmony and ease, in short, by which with us the work is apt to be accompanied, and from which a European who should do the same work would nine times out of ten be free. . . . It is your relaxed and easy worker, who is in no hurry, and quite thoughtless most of the while of consequences, who is your efficient worker; and tension and anxiety, and present and future, all mixed up together in one mind at once, are the surest drags upon steady progress and hindrances to our success."—``Talks to Teachers," pp. 214- 218.

Mr. Joseph Lyons, who is recognized as one of the particularly active and efficient men of England, has taken great interest in the way things are done in America. And after ob- <p 209> serving us at work here he expressed himself as dissatisfied with the tension under which we work. His words areas follows:—

``I do not believe in what Americans call hustling. The American hustler in my opinion does not represent the highest type of human efficiency. He wastes a lot of nervous power and energy instead of accomplishing the greatest possible amount of work for the force expended. Judging the American hustler from my observation of him in his own country, I should say that the American hustler shows a lack of adaptation of means to ends because he puts more mental, physical, and nervous energy into his work at all times than it demands. Regarded as a machine he is not an economical one. He breaks down too often and has to be laid off for repairs too often. He tries to do everything too fast."

When Mr. Lyons was asked to explain how he had been able to accomplish so much without hustling, he replied: ``By organizing myself to run smoothly as well as my business; by schooling myself to keep cool, and to do <p 210> what I have to do without expending more nervous energy on the task than is necessary; by avoiding all needless friction. In consequence, when I finish my day's work, I feel nearly as fresh as when I started."— Quoted from *New York Herald,* Aug. 30, 1910.

RELAXATION A PHYSIOLOGICAL NECESSITY

The necessity for relaxation is adherent in the human organism. Even those life processes which seem to be constant in their activity require frequent periods of complete rest.

The heart beats regularly and at short intervals, but after each beat its muscles come into a state of complete relaxation and enjoy a refreshing rest, even though it be but for a moment. Likewise the lungs seem to be unceasing in their activity, but a careful study of their action discloses the fact that every contraction is followed by a perfect relaxation, and that the rest secured between successive respirations is adequate for recuperations.

In all bodily processes the same alternation is discovered. No bodily activity is at all con- <p 211> tinuous. Mental processes, too, can be continued for but a very short time. By attempting to eliminate these periods of rest for bodily and mental acts, we merely exhaust without a corresponding increase in efficiency. The laws of nature are firm and countenance no infringement.

The periods between activity and rest, as well as the durations of the two processes, may be changed. Thus, up to a certain limit, the periods devoted to activity may follow more rapidly and endure longer. There is, however, a danger point which may not be passed with impunity. The danger signal may manifest itself in several ways: The over- trained athlete becomes ``stale''; the over- worked brain worker becomes nervous; the overworked laborer becomes indifferent and generally inefficient.

In all these and in similar instances, the amount of energy expended is out of proportion to the results of the labor. The athletic trainer has learned to guard against overtraining and is severely condemned for making <p 212> such a mistake. The brain worker often regards overwork as a commendable thing. However, sentiment is changing. The employer of labor is finding that rest and relaxation are essential to the greatest efficiency. Employees accomplish as much in a week of six days as they do in one of seven. The reduction in the hours of daily toil has not decreased the total efficiency.

The periods devoted to rest are not as profitable as they should be unless they are actually devoted to recuperation. It may be that some of the time supposed to be devoted to rest should be devoted to thoughts of toil. Again during the hours of work there should be a freedom from jerkiness, breathlessness, nervousness, and anxiety. It is not necessarily true that the greatest and most constant display of energy accompanies the greatest presence of energy. The tugboat in the river is constantly blowing off steam and making a tremendous display of energy, while the ocean liner proceeds on its way without noise and without commotion. The still current runs <p 213> deep, and the man who is actually accomplishing the most is frequently—perhaps always the man who is making the least display of his strength. He can afford to be calm and collected, for he is equal to his task. The man who frets and fumes, who is nervous and excited, who is strung up to such a pitch that energy is being dissipated in all directions— such a man proclaims his weakness from the housetop.

Many business men know they are going at a pace that kills, and at the same time they feel that they are accomplishing too little. For such, the pertinent question is, How may I reduce the expenditure of energy without reducing the efficiency of my labor?

The ability to relax at will and to remain in an efficient condition, but free from nervousness, is a thing which may be acquired more or less completely by all persons. It is accomplished by a voluntary control of the muscles of the arms, legs, and face, by breathing slowly and deeply, and by placing the body in a condition of general relaxation. <p 214>

This antecedent condition of relaxation brings all the forces of the mind and body more completely under control and makes it possible to marshal them more effectively. It also gives one a feeling of control and assurance, which minimizes the possibility of confusion and embarrassment in the presence of an important task. The possibility of developing the power of relaxation by means of special training is being taken advantage of in teaching acts of skill, in all forms of mental therapeutics, and in numerous other instances where overtension hinders the acquisition or accomplishment of a useful act. By assuming the attitude of assurance and composure, the actual condition is produced in a manner most astonishing to those who have never attempted it. No man can do his best when he is hurried and fearful, when he is expending energy in a manner as useless as a tug blowing off steam. That relief is within his own power seems to him impossible. He is not aware of his power of will to change from his state of anxiety to one of composure. <p 215>

That the gospel of relaxation is more important to the chief executive than to the day laborer is quite apparent. Even in the case of the day laborer the crack of the lash and the curse of the driver may have been capable of securing a display of activity among the laborers, but such means are not comparable in efficiency to the more modern methods. Laborers are now given more hours of rest, are not kept fearful and anxious, but are given short hours of labor and long hours of rest. They are judged by the actual results of their labor rather than by their apparent activity.

When accomplishing intellectual work of any sort, it is found that worry exhausts more than labor.

Anxiety as to the results is detrimental to efficiency. The intellectual worker should periodically make it a point to sit in his chair with the muscles of his legs relaxed, to breathe deeply, and to assume an attitude of composure. Such an attitude must not, of course, detract from attention to the work at hand, but should rather increase it. Upon leaving <p 216> his office, the brain worker should cultivate the habit of forgetting all about his business, except in so far as he believes that some particular point needs special attention out of office hours. The habit of brooding over business is detrimental to efficiency and is also suicidal to the individual.

It is, of course, apparent to all that relaxation may mean permanent indifference, and such a condition is infinitely worse than too great a tension. An employer who is never keyed up to his work, and an employee who goes about his work in an indifferent manner, are not regarded in the present discussion.

A complete relaxation of the body often gives freedom to the intellect. The inventor is often able, when lying in bed, to devise his apparatus with a perfection impossible when he attempts to study it out in the shop. The forgotten name will not come till we cease straining for it. Very many of the world's famous poems have been conceived while the poet was lying in an easy and relaxed condition. This fact is so well recognized by some <p 217> authors that they voluntarily go to bed in the daytime and get perfectly relaxed in order that their minds may do the most perfect work. Much constructive thinking is done in the quiet of the sanctuary, when the monotony of the liturgy or the voice of the speaker has soothed the quiet nerves, and secured a composed condition of mind. The preacher would be surprised if he knew how many costumes had been planned, how many business ventures had been outlined, all because of the soothing influence of his words.

This relaxation of the body not only gives freedom to the intellect, but it is the necessary preliminary condition for the greatest physical exertion and for the most perfect execution of any series of skillful acts.

Mr. H. L. Doherty not only held the world's championship in tennis, but he was the despair of his opponents, because of the apparent lack of exertion which he put forth to meet their volleys. So far as an observer could judge, Mr. Doherty kept only those muscles tense that were used in the game. The muscles <p 218> especially necessary for tennis were also, so far as possible, kept lax except at the instant for making the stroke. Partly because of this relaxation, his muscles were free from exhaustion and under such perfect control that at the critical moment he was able to exert a strength that was tremendous and a skill that was amazing.

In a very striking paragraph Professor James has shown the reason why poise and efficiency of mind are incompatible with tenseness of muscles:—

``By the sensations that so incessantly pour in from the overtense excited body the overtense and excited habit of mind is kept up; and the sultry, threatening, exhausting, thunderous inner atmosphere never quite clears away. If you never give yourself up wholly to the chair you sit in, but always keep your leg and body muscles half contracted for a rise; if you breathe eighteen or nineteen instead of sixteen times a minute, and never quite breathe out at that,—what mental mood can you be in but one of inner panting and expectancy, and how <p 219> can the future and its worries possibly forsake your mind? On the other hand, how can they gain admission to your mind if your brow be unruffled, your respiration calm and complete, and your muscles all relaxed?"—``Talks to Teachers," p. 211.

In ancient Greece, one of the chief functions of the school was to prepare citizens to profit by the hours of freedom from toil. Herbert Spencer, in his great work on Education, gives a prominent place to training for leisure hours. Such training is attracting the attention of the American educator to-day as never before. A few decades ago the majority of the American population lived on farms, spent long hours of the day in toil, and scarcely thought of recreation. We have now become an urban population, the hours of labor have been greatly reduced during the days of the week, and Sunday is a day in which the laborer is found in neither the factory nor the church.

The employer of laborers fears the effect of long hours of freedom from toil. He has prophesied that such hours would be spent <p 220> in dissipations. He feared that as a result his laborers would enter their shops with unsteady hands and sleepy brains. That such results are all too often due to freedom from toil, no one would deny. That they are not necessary will also be admitted. One of the problems of the American people as a whole, and of employers of labor in particular, is to train up the rising generations so that they may make the best use of the increasing hours of freedom from labor.

To this end the schools are doing much. Settlement workers are contributing their part. Welfare work is becoming popular in certain places. Local clubs are being organized to develop interest in local improvement, literature, politics, ethics, religion, music, athletics. These agencies are so beneficial in results that they are being generously encouraged by business men.

Upon entering business every young man should select some form of endeavor or activity apart from business to which he shall devote a part of his attention. This interest should be so <p 221> absorbing that when he is thus engaged, business is banished from mind.

This interest may be a home and a family; it may be some form of athletics; it may be club life; it may be art, literature, philanthropy, or religion. It must be something which appeals to the individual and is adapted to his capabilities. Some men find it advisable to have more than a single interest for the hours of recreation. Some form of athletics or of agriculture is often combined with an interest in art, literature, religion, or other intellectual form of recreation. Thus Gladstone is depicted as a woodchopper and as an author of Greek works. Carnegie is described as an enthusiast in golf and in philanthropy. Rockefeller is believed to be interested in golf and philanthropy, but his philanthropy takes the form of education through endowed schools. Carnegie's philanthropy is in building libraries. If the lives of the great business men are studied it will be found that there is a great diversity in the type of recreation chosen; but philanthropy, religion, and athletics are <p 222> very prominent—perhaps the most popular of the outside interests.

These interests cannot be suddenly acquired. Many a man who has reached the years of maturity has found to his sorrow that he is without interests in the world except his specialty or business. With each succeeding year he finds new interests more difficult to acquire. Hence young men should in their youth choose wisely some interests to which they may devote themselves with perfect abandon at more or less regular intervals throughout life.

The more noble and the more worthy the interest, the better will be the results when considered from any point of view. Indeed, the interests which we call the highest are properly so designated, because in the history of mankind they have proved themselves to be the most beneficial to all.

CHAPTER X

THE RATE OF IMPROVEMENT IN EFFICIENCY

NO novice develops suddenly into an expert. Nevertheless the progress made by beginners is often astounding. The executive with experience is not deceived by the showing made by new men. He has learned to accept rapid initial progress, but he does not assume that this initial rate of increase will be sustained.

The rate at which skill is acquired has been the subject of many careful studies. The results have been charted and reduced to curves, variously spoken of as ``efficiency curves,'' ``practice curves,'' ``learning curves,'' according to the nature of the task or test. Some of these dealt with the routine work of office and factory. In others typical muscular and mental activities were observed in a simpler form than could be found in actual practice. <p 223> <p 224>

Five of my advanced students joined me in strenuous practice in adding columns of figures for a few minutes daily for a month. Our task was to add 765 one-place figures daily in the shortest possible time. No emphasis was placed on accuracy, but each one tried to make

{illust. caption = FIG. 1.}

the highest daily record for speed. The results of our practice are graphically shown in Curve A of Fig. 1. As shown in that curve for the first day our average speed was only forty-two combinations per minute, but for the thirtieth day our average was seventy-four combinations per minute, We did not quite <p 225> double our speed by the practice, and we made but little improvement in accuracy. The most rapid gain was, as anticipated, during the first few days. We made but little progress from the sixteenth to the twenty-third day, and also from the twenty-fourth to the thirtieth day.

Of the six persons practicing addition, five of us also practiced the making of a maximum grip with a thumb and forefinger. Just before beginning the adding each day this maximum grip (or pinch) was exerted once a second for sixty seconds, first with the right hand and then with the left. Likewise at the completion of the addition sixty grips were taken by the right hand and sixty by the left. The total pressure exerted by each individual in the 240 trials (four minutes) was then recorded and expressed in kilograms. The result of the experiment is shown in curve B of Fig. 1. The average total pressure for each of the five persons was for the first day 620 kilograms; for the twenty-fourth day 1400 kilograms. Our increase was very rapid for the <p 226> first few days, and no general slump was encountered till the last week of practice. In one particular our results in the test on physical strength were not anticipated—we did not suppose that by practicing four minutes daily for thirty days we could double our physical strength in any such a series of maximum grips with the thumb and forefinger.

It is a simple matter to measure day by day the accomplishment of one learning to use the typewriter. All beginners who take the work seriously and work industriously pass through similar stages in this learning process. Figure 2 represents the record for the first eighty- six days of a learner who was devoting, in all, sixty minutes daily to actual writing. The numbers to the left of the figure in the vertical column indicate the number of strokes (including punctuations and shifts) made in ten minutes. The numbers on the base line indicate the days of practice. Thus on the ninth day the learner wrote 700 strokes in the ten minutes; on the fifty-fourth day 1300 strokes; on the eighty-sixth day over 1400 strokes. <p 227>

Figure 3 represents the results of a writer of some little experience who spent one hour a day writing a special form of copy.

In this curve it will be observed that the

{illust. caption = FIG. 2.}

increase in efficiency was very great during the first few weeks, but that during the succeeding weeks little improvement was made.—BOOK, W. R, ``The Psychology of Skill," p. 20. <p 228>

The progress of a telegraph operator is determined by the number of words which he

{illust. caption = FIG. 3.}

can send or receive with accuracy per minute. In learning telegraphy, progress is rapid for a few weeks and then follow many weeks of less rapid improvement. Figure 4 presents the <p 229 history of a student of telegraphy who was devoting all his time to sending and receiving messages. His speed was measured once a week from his first week to the time when he

{illust. caption = FIG. 4.}

could be classed as a fully accomplished operator. By the twentieth week this operator could receive less than 70 letters a minute, although he could send over 120 letters a minute. At the end of the fortieth week he had <p 230> reached a speed of sending which he would probably never greatly excel even though his speed was far below that attained by many operators. The receiving rate might possibly rise either slowly or rapidly until it equaled or exceeded the sending rate.—BRYAN & HARTER, ``Studies in the Physiology and Psychology of the Telegraphic Language," *Psychological Review*, Vol. IV, p. 49.

There are certain forms of learning and practice which do not readily admit of quantitative determinations. Nevertheless very successful attempts have been made even in the most difficult realms of learning. A beginner with the Russian language spent 30 minutes daily in industrious study and then was tested for 15 minutes as to the number of Russian words he could translate. Figure 5 shows diagrammatically the results of the experiment. Thus on the thirteenth day 22 words were translated; on the fiftieth day 45 words. Improvement was rather rapid until the nineteenth day, and then followed a slump till the forty-sixth day. Improvement was very ir- <p 231> regular.—SWIFT, E. J., ``Mind in the Making," p. 198.

These five figures are typical of nearly all

{illust. caption = FIG. 5.}

practice, or learning, curves. They depict the rate at which the beginner increases his efficiency. In every case we discover very great <p 232> fluctuations. On one day or at one moment there is a sudden phenomenal improvement. The next day or even the next moment the increase may be lost and a return made to a lower stage of efficiency.

There are certain forms of skill which cannot be acquired rapidly in the beginning. In such instances a period of time is necessary in which to ``warm up" or in which to acquire the knack of the operation or the necessary degree of familiarity and self-confidence before improvement becomes possible. This is true particularly in the ``breaking in" of new operators on large machines like steam hammers, cranes, and the like, where the mass and power of the machine awes the new man, even though he has had experience with smaller units of some kind. It applies also to new inspectors of mechanical parts and completed products in factories—

especially where the factor of judgment enters into the operation. Such instances are exceptions, however, and differ from those cited only in having a period of slow advance preliminary to the rapid progress. <p 233>

Apparently, improvement should be continuous until the learner has entered into the class of experts or has reached his possible maximum. As a matter of fact the curve which expresses his advance towards efficiency never rises steadily from a low degree to a high one. Periods of improvement are universally followed by stages of stagnation or retrogression. These periods of little or no improvement following periods of rapid improvement are called ``plateaus" and are found in the experience of all who are acquiring skill in any line.

These plateaus are not all due to the same cause.

They differ somewhat with individuals and even more with the nature of the task in which skill is being acquired. With all, however, the following four factors are the most important influence:—

1. *The enthusiasm dependent upon novelty becomes exhausted.*

2. *All easy improvements have been made.*

3. *A period of ``incubation" is needed in* <p 234> *which the new habits under formation may have time to develop.*

4. *Voluntary attention cannot be sustained for a long period of time.*

These four factors are not only the causes of the first plateau, but, as soon as any particular plateau is overcome and advance again begun, they are likely to arrest the advance and to cause another period of recession or of no advance. These four factors are therefore most significant to every man who is trying to increase his own efficiency or promote the progress of others.

When the interest in work is dependent on novelty, the plateau comes early in the development, and further progress is possible only by the injection of new motives to action.

Many young persons begin things with enthusiasm, but drop them when the novelty has worn off. They develop no stable interests and in all their tasks are superficial. They often have great potential ability, but lack training in habits of industry and of continued application. They change positions <p 235> often, acquire much diversified experience, and frequently, in a new position, give promise of developing unusual skill or ability. This is due to the fact that during the first weeks or months of their new employment the novelty of the work stimulates them to activity, and the methods or habits learned in other trades are available for application to the new tasks. When the novelty wears off, however, they become wearied and cast about for a fresh and therefore more alluring field. Such nomads prove unprofitable employees even when they are the means of introducing new methods or short cuts into a business. They strike a plateau and lose interest and initiative just at the point where more industrious and less superficial men would begin to be of the greatest value.

Plateaus are not confined to clerks and other subordinates. Executives frequently ``go stale" on their jobs and lose their accustomed energy and initiative. Sometimes they are able to diagnose their own condition and provide the corrective stimulus. Again the <p 236> man higher up, if he has the wisdom and discernment which some gain from experience, observes the situation and prescribes for his troubled lieutenant. In the majority of cases, however, the occupant of a plateau, if he continues thereon for any length of time, either resigns despondent or is dismissed.

Such a case, coming under my notice recently, illustrates the man-losses suffered by organizations whose heads do not realize that salaries alone will not buy efficiency.

A young advertising man had almost grown up with his house, coming to it when not yet twenty in a minor position in the sales department. Enthusiastic about his possibilities, with the friendship and co<o:>peration of his immediate superior, he carried out well the successive duties put to him. Promotion was rapid. No position was retained more than six months. In five years he had occupied nearly every subordinate position in the sales department, and was promoted to the head of the mail-order section. <p 237>

His fertility in originating plans, his schemes, his booklets, and advertising copy brought results with regularity. He became known as a man who could ``put the thing over" in a pinch, with a vigor and enthusiasm that seemed irresistible. He fairly earned his standing as the live wire among executives of the second rank.

So, when the general sales manager resigned, there was no question but that this young man should succeed him. He had been a personal friend of his predecessor, had co<o:>perated with him in many phases of his work, and knew his new duties well; in fact, he took them up with little necessity for ``breaking in."

This apparently favorable condition was the very reason for his lack of success in the new work. There was not the novelty in this position that there had been in his former successive positions. In such an executive position, it was not a question of taking care of an emergency demand, but of organization, of establishing routine, of organizing bigger campaigns. Before the end of the first season it became evi- <p 238> dent that the new sales manager was not making good. Everything—organization, discipline, routine system, ginger—had deserted him. Neither he himself nor his employers, however, found the real cause. ``I have lost my grip," he told the general manager. ``I am worn out and of no further use to this business."

Furthermore he thought he was of no use to any business. But he made a connection with a big house which had a large advertising campaign on its hands. He threw himself into the task of recasting the firm's selling literature, the planning of new campaigns, and the reorganization of the correspondence department. Within the year, he had duplicated on a magnified scale his early triumphs with his first employers. Moreover, he continued this record of efficiency the second year, thus entirely refuting the fear of himself and his friends that he would ``last less than a year" and that he lacked staying power.

His first employer described the case for me <p 239> the other day, requesting that I discover the reason for the young man's initial failure among friends and his subsequent triumph in a new environment. He had kept in close touch with the other's progress and supplied a hundred details which helped to make the situation clear. Finally, after consideration, he agreed with my diagnosis that his young friend's falling off in efficiency— his plateau—had been due to the exhaustion of novelty interest in his work.

His first success was built on a long series of separate plans or ``stunts," each of which was begun and executed in a burst of creative enthusiasm. His first few months' achievement as sales manager was due to the same stimulus, but as the months went by the spur of novelty became dulled. Lacking the discipline which would have enabled him to force voluntary attention and the resulting interest in his tasks, he failed also to trace the cause of his flagging invention and energy and assumed that this was due to exhaustion of his resources. <p 240>

This is further borne out by his experience in his present position. Addressing a succession of new tasks, the interest of novelty has stimulated him to an uncommon degree and produced an unbroken record of high efficiency. That this has continued over a considerable period is partly due, beyond doubt, to the sustained interest in his work excited by the broadness of the field before him, the bigness of the company, the size of the appropriation at his disposal, the unusual experience of scoring hit after hit by comparison with the house's low standards, the frank and prompt appreciation of his superiors, and substantial advances in salary.

It is only human to be more or less dependent upon novelty. If I am to stir myself to continuous and effective exertion, I must frequently stimulate my interest by proposing new problems and new aspects of my work. If I am to help others to increase their efficiency, I must devise new appeals to their interest and new stimulations to action. If I have been dependent upon competition as a stimulus <p 241> I must change the form of the contest—a fact which receives daily recognition and application by the most efficient sales organization in the country. If I have been depending upon the stimulating effect of wages, there is profit occasionally in varying the method of payment or in furnishing some new concrete measure of the value of the wage. To the average worker, for example, a check means much less than the same amount in gold. In deference to this common appreciation of ``cold cash,'' various firms have lately abandoned checks and pay in gold and banknotes, even though this change means many hours of extra work for the cashier.

At every stage of our learning, progress is aided by the utilization of old habits and old fragments of knowledge.

In learning to add, the schoolboy employs his previous knowledge of numbers. In learning to multiply he builds upon his acquaintance with addition and subtraction. In solving problems in percentage his success is measured by the freedom with which he can <p 242> use the four fundamental processes of addition, subtraction, Multiplication, and division. In computing bank discount, his skill is based on ability to employ his previous experience with percentage and the fundamental processes of arithmetic.

The advance here is typical of all learning processes. In mastering the typewriter no absolutely new movement is required. The old familiar movements of arm and hand are united in new combinations. The student has previously learned the letters found in the copy and can identify them upon the keys of the typewriter. Scrutiny enables him to find any particular key, and in the course of a few hours be develops a certain awkward familiarity with the keyboard and acquires some speed by utilizing these familiar muscular movements and available bits of knowledge. All these prelearned movements and associations are brought into service in the early stages of improvement, and a degree of proficiency is quickly attained which cannot be exceeded so long as these prelearned habits and asso- <p 243> ciations alone are employed. Further advance in speed and accuracy is dependent upon combinations more difficult to make because they involve organization of the old and acquisition of new methods of thought or movement. When such a difficulty is faced, a plateau in the learning curve is almost inevitable.

The young man who enters upon the work of a salesman can make immediate use of a multitude of previous habits and previously acquired bits of knowledge. He performs by habit all the ordinary movements of the body; by habit he speaks, reads, and writes. During his previous experience he has acquired some skill in judging people, in addressing them, and in influencing them. His general information and his practice in debate and conversation— however crude—enable him to analyze his selling proposition and unite these selling points into an argument. He learns, too, to avoid certain errors and to make use of certain factors of his previous experience. Thus his progress is rapid for a short time but soon <p 244> the stage is reached where his previous experience offers no more factors which can be easily brought to his service. In such an emergency the novice may cease to advance—if indeed there is not a positive retrogression.

Nor is this tendency to strike a plateau confined to clerks in the office and to semi- skilled men in the factory. Often the limitations of a new executive are brought out sharply by his failure to handle a situation much less difficult than scores which he has already mastered and thereby built up a reputation for unusual efficiency. His collapse, when analyzed, can usually be traced to the fact that his previous experience contained nothing on which he could directly base a decision. His prior efficiency was based on empirical knowledge rather than on judgment or ability to analyze problems.

The office manager of an important mercantile house is a case in point. Though young, he had served several companies in the same capacity, making a distinct advance at each change. He was a trained accountant, <p 245> a clever employment man, and a successful handler of men and women. His association with the various organizations from which he had graduated gave him an unusual fund of practical knowledge and tried-out methods to draw upon.

His first six months were starred with brilliant detail reorganizations. The shipping department, first; the correspondence division next; the accounting department third, and he literally swept through the office like the proverbial new broom, caught up all the loose ends, and established a routine like clockwork. So successful was his work that the directors hastened to add supervision of sales and collections.

Forthwith the new manager struck his plateau. His previous experience offered little he could readily use in shaping a sales policy or laying out a collection program. He plunged into the details of both, effected some important minor economies, but failed altogether —as subsequent events showed—to grasp the constructive needs and opportunities <p 246> of management. He puzzled and irritated his district managers by overemphasizing details when they wanted decisions or policies or help in handling sales emergencies. In the same way, he neglected collections,—chiefly because he could not distinguish between detail and questions of policy,—but escaped blame for more than six months because the season was conceded to be a poor one.

Not till he resigned and the general manager investigated the sales and collection departments did the real cause of the failure become evident. Important and numerous as had been the economics instituted, they all fell under the head of the ``easy improvements " based on previous experience and observation. When problems outside this experience presented themselves, the manager encountered his plateau.

In the acquisition of skill, days of progress are followed by stationary periods. ``Time must be taken out" to allow the formation of a habit or the organization of this new knowledge or skill. <p 247>

All trees and plants have periods of growth followed by periods of little or no growth. In May and June the leaves and branches shoot forth very rapidly, but the new growth is pulpy and tender. During succeeding days or months, these tender shots are filled in and developed. In learning and in habit formation a similar sequence is lived through. We have days of swift advancement followed by days in which the new stage or method of thinking and acting takes time to become organized and solidified. The nervous system has to adjust itself to the new demands, and such adjusting requires time.

Although periods of incubation are essential for every specific habit, practically every act of skill is dependent upon a number of simpler habits. At any one time progress may be made in utilizing some of these habits, even though others could not be advantageously hastened. Thus the period of incubation should not necessarily cause any profound slump in the advance. Almost invariably, however, it produces a plateau which persists until the worker <p 248> has mastered the expert way. The golf player, for example, usually finds he is able to drive longer and straighter balls at the beginning of the season than a little later. The reason is that in golf the perfect stroke is the product of almost automatic muscular action. In the first round the swing of the driver or iron is not consciously governed, and the muscular habit of the previous year controls. Later, as the player concentrates on his task of correcting little faults or learning more effective methods, his stroke loses its automatic quality, his game falls off, and it is not until he masters his new form that he attains high efficiency.

The same cycle is repeated in office and factory operations, where efficiency is possible only when the hands carry out automatically the desired action. In typewriting and telegraphy, in the handling of adding machines, in the feeding of drill presses, punch presses, and hundreds of special machines, the learner passes through three distinct phases: first, swift improvement in which prelearned move- <p 249> ments and skill are brought to bear on the task under the stimulus of both novelty interest and voluntary interest; second, arrested progress— the period of incubation or habit formation; and the final stage of automatic skill and efficiency.

Since increase of efficiency is dependent upon continued efforts of will, slumps are inevitable. Voluntary attention cannot be sustained for a long period.

Work requiring effort is always subject to fluctuations. The man with a strong will may make the lapses in attention relatively short. He may be on his guard and ``try to try" most faithfully, but no exertion of the will can keep up a steady expenditure of effort in any single activity. All significant *increases* in efficiency, however, are dependent upon voluntary attention—upon extreme exertions of the will.

No man can develop into an expert without great exertion of the will. Such exertions of the will are recognized by authorities as being very exhaustive and unstable. One of the greatest of the authorities and one who in <p 250> particular has emphasized the necessity of a ``do-or-die" attitude of work concludes his discussion with the following significant admission: ``All this suggests that if one wants to improve at the most rapid rate, he must work when he can feel good and succeed, then lounge and wait until it is again profitable to work. It is when all the conditions are favorable that the forward steps or new adaptations are made."

Voluntary attention must be employed in making the advance step, in improving our method of work, and in making any sort of helpful changes. But voluntary attention must not be depended upon to secure steady and continuous utilization of the improved method or rate of work. To secure this end, an attempt should be made to reduce the work to habit so far as possible and also to secure spontaneous interest either from interest and pleasure in the work itself or because of the reward to be received.

The case of the young sales manager, described in the first part of this article, suggests <p 251> some of the methods by which this interest can be secured. The chief factor in his progress was the interest in the work itself due to the novelty of his successive tasks—an element impossible to introduce into the average man's job. Yet there were other and powerful motives stimulating his interest: the responsibility of organizing a big department and of directing the expenditure of large sums of money; the prompt credit given him and the growing confidence extended to him; and the expression of their appreciation in the concrete shape of salary increases.

It is quite true that these various stimulating factors cannot be produced indefinitely; tasks must ``stale,'' praise grow monotonous, salaries touch their top level. But ``making good'' and finding interests in work crystallize into habits which endure as long as conditions remain fair. The rise of the efficiency curve thus depends upon recurrent periods of successful struggle followed by periods of habit formation and by the development of powerful spontaneous interests. <p 252>

Voluntary interest is a valuable thing to possess, but a difficult thing to secure either within ourselves or in those under our charge.

In its psychological aspect, scientific management enters here. By working out and establishing a standard method and standard time for various ``repeat'' operations a workman is engaged in, it encourages—and even enforces—the formation of new efficiency habits. The bonus paid for the accomplishment of the task in the specified time supplies an immediate and powerful motive to the effort necessary to master the ``right way'' of doing things.

In the main, employees do their best to acquire efficiency; but their humanness must not be forgotten, and the burden of increasing efficiency must be carried largely by the executive. His part it is to supply interest, if the nature of the work forbids the finding of it there, he must introduce it from outside either by competition, by emphasizing the connection between the task and the reward, as in piecework, or by provision of a bonus <p 253> for the achievement of a certain standard of efficiency.

He must eliminate the factors in environment or organization which distract employees and make voluntary interest more difficult. He must provide the means of training and must understand the possibilities and the limitations of training. If a man ``slumps'' in efficiency, he must look for the cause and make sure this is not beyond the man's control before he punishes him. In a word, he must allow for periods of incubation or unconscious organization before expecting maximum results from a new employee or an old man assigned to a new job.

The man who by persistent effort has developed himself into an expert has greatly enhanced his value to society. The boss who demands expert service from untrained men is either a tyrant or a fool. But the executive who develops novices into experts and the company which transforms mere ``handy men'' into mechanics are public benefactors because of the service rendered to the country and their men.

CHAPTER XI

PRACTICE PLUS THEORY

THE demand for trained and experienced men is never supplied. Most business and industrial organizations find their growth impeded by the dearth of such men. To employ men trained by competitors or by inferior organizations is expensive and unsatisfactory. A man trained till he has become valuable to his ``parent'' organization is not likely to be equally valuable to other organizations that might employ him at a later time. In general, the most valuable men in any organization are the men who have grown up in it.

The man who is ``a rolling stone" secures, in a way, more experience than the man who is developed within a single organization, but his wider experience does not of necessity make him a more valuable man. It is not mere <p 254> <p 255> experience that educates, develops, and equips men, but experience of particular sorts, and acquired under very well defined conditions.

``Scientific management" has taken seriously the problem of providing and utilizing the most valuable experiences. But the viewpoint of the leaders in this modern movement is that of the employer seeking the most valuable experiences for those employees whose work is mainly mechanical, *e.g.* machine tenders, stenographers, etc. Scientific management has conclusively demonstrated the fact that it is poor economy to depend upon haphazard experiences for the development of those employees whose excellence depends upon the speed and accuracy of their occupation habits. It has thus done great service in demonstrating the kind of experience most valuable in developing men for positions of routine work. But it has done little for men whose welfare depends upon judgment —in making new adjustments and in solving the new problems continually arising in all positions of responsibility. It has left for others <p 256> to consider the experiences most profitable for developing executives.

The most valuable experience in acquiring an act of skill is frequent repetition in performing the act.

The value of the experience continues till by frequent repetition the act has become so mechanical that it is performed without attention. Further experience has little or no value.

On the other hand it is true that every worthy calling demands forms of activity which could not and should not be mechanized. There are emergencies in every form of occupation that call for new adjustments. The ability to make such new adjustments depends upon richness of experience and width of view as well as upon skill in performing the old processes.

The difference between a machine and a man is that the man is capable of adjusting himself to the changed situation, while a machine cannot do so. The machine may work more accurately and more rapidly than the man <p 257> in routine work, but it is capable of nothing but routine work. There is a need for much experience to make the man approximate the skill and accuracy obtained by a machine. But there is also need of experience to develop the man in that particular in which he surpasses a machine, *i.e.* in a broad experience that enables him to form judgments and hence to make a multitude of different adjustments when a need for a change occurs.

A machine is constructed to perform a particular kind of routine work in a stereotyped way, but so soon as there is discovered a better way of performing this work the machine is thrown to the scrap heap because it cannot be adjusted to new requirements.

Experience which renders human activity machine-like is a form of experience that increases the probability that the possessor will be discarded and his work accomplished by the introduction of some new tool or some new method of work.

Experience therefore which merely increases the skill of action without increasing the width <p 258> of horizon is necessary, but it is inadequate. In addition to skill in routine work the man should secure the broader experience that will enable him to adjust himself to changed conditions in his occupation and that will develop the judgment necessary to enable him to adjust his vocation to new demands. Every form of occupation has many possibilities, a few of which are from time to time discovered to be significant. Advance in any sphere of work depends upon the discovery of these possibilities which the untrained eye of inexperience does not detect.

Although a broad experience may enable the man to grasp the possibilities of his occupation, it fails to secure skill in the particulars that have already been found to be important. While a broad experience leaves a man incapable of present competition, the narrow experience jeopardizes his future.

The most valuable experience is therefore one that equips the man to compete with the skillful in the present and to comprehend his task so that he may from time to time adjust <p 259> it to new relationships. It emphasizes the formation of necessary habits, but does not neglect the development of the judgment. Such an experience is both intensive and extensive; informal and formal; mechanical and theoretical; practical and scientific. Such experience alone meets the demands of the increasing complexity of industrial and commercial life.

HOW MAY THE MOST VALUABLE EXPERIENCE BE SECURED AND UTILIZED

I. Haphazard Experience

But little attention is given to providing those experiences that most adequately prepare one for commercial and industrial life. The boy who is to become a skilled workman is compelled to ``pick up" his experience as best he can. The same is true of the boy who aspires to a position as salesman, banker, or manufacturer. Every employer seeks only experienced men, and but few places are available where such experience can be economically and honorably secured. <p 260>

The youth without experience, desiring to become a skilled machinist, may secure some experience with machinery in a second-rate factory during the rush season. Because of his incapacity, he is laid off as soon as the rush is over. Thereupon he applies as an experienced machinist in a better shop. If he is lucky, he may secure a position. If the supervision is inadequate, or the demand for labor unusual, he may retain his position for several hours, or days, or even weeks. After years of such distressing experiences, the youth succeeds in ``stealing his trade." In the meantime he has been an economic loss to his many employers, and his experience may have depraved his character.

The condition found in the industrial world is no worse than that in the commercial world. The selling force is recuperated by green hands. In most selling organizations no instruction is given and no experience provided except what is picked up haphazard behind the counter or on the road. Most new men fail, are dismissed, employed by another firm and dis- <p 261> missed again, etc. We have here nothing but a struggle for existence and the survival of the fittest in a crude and destructive form.

The burnt child avoids the fire, and his experience is most effective. However, the wise parent arranges conditions so that the burn shall not be too serious. The machinist who ``steals" his trade profits greatly by his mistakes, and the new salesman never forgets some of his most flagrant errors. Such experiences are practical, lasting, effective, but uneconomical. But such experiences are of necessity unsystematic and inadequate to modern industrial and commercial demands.

II. Apprenticeship Experience

The waste in the Haphazard method of securing experience in the industrial world has long been apparent and has led to attempts to provide systems of apprenticeships which would enable the youth to secure educative experiences with a minimum of cost to himself and his employer.

In theory the youth who becomes an ap- <p 262> prentice is bound or indentured to serve his master for a period of years. During that time the master agrees to see to it that the apprentice practices and becomes proficient in performing all the processes of the trade. The employer (master) is rewarded in that he secures the continuous service of the boy for the period of years upon the payment of little or no wages. Furthermore the apprentice when developed into a journeyman is likely to become a valuable employee. The apprentice is rewarded for his years of service by the practical experience which he has been permitted to secure in actual work with all the various processes involved in the trade.

Although the apprenticeship system has many excellent points, it has been found inadequate to meet the needs of modern commercial and industrial institutions. At least in its primitive form it is decadent in every industry which has been modernized. All forms of commerce and industry have become so complicated and each part demands such perfection of skill that an apprentice can <p 263> scarcely secure sufficient experience in even the essentials of the trade to render him expert in these various processes. In short, the traditional apprenticeship system is unable to give either the general comprehension of the industry or the skill in the specialized processes.

III. Theoretical-practical Experience

In contrast with the two methods discussed above (Haphazard Experience and Apprenticeship Experience) schools must be considered as a method of providing experiences preparatory to industrial life. The first two methods secure skill, but the schools secure learning. The first two might be said to educate the hands and the latter the head. The comparative advantages of these contrasted systems is the theme of unceasing debate. The man skilled in one thing can at least do that one thing well. The man who is learned but not skilled in any activity of his chosen occupation is unable to compete with the boys who at the expense of schooling, ``went to work'' in that particular occupation. <p 264>

An advanced general school education has very distinct advantages. But skill in reading Latin does not greatly increase one's ability to read instruments of precision. Skill in applying mathematical formul<ae> will not greatly assist in estimating the value of merchandise. A knowledge of general psychology will not insure ability in selecting employees. Even great proficiency in discoursing upon ethical theories does not protect one from the temptation to be dishonest in business.

Skill in one thing does not insure skill in other and even in similar things. Learning in one field is not incompatible with gross ignorance in other and related fields. We have discovered that skill and learning are largely specialized, and accordingly we see the necessity of acquiring skill and learning in the particular fields in which the skill and learning are desired. To meet these demands various modifications in our schools have been made. To meet the needs of training for the industries we have the manual training schools, industrial schools, trade schools, continuation <p 265> schools, correspondence schools, night schools, technological schools, etc. To provide the appropriate experiences for commercial life we have commercial schools, business colleges, store schools, schools of commerce, etc.

These schools have rendered invaluable service and are rapidly increasing in number, yet they do not provide either the skill or the learning which should be possessed by the employee.

IV. Practical-theoretical Experience

The weakness of the Haphazard and Apprenticeship methods of securing experience is twofold: (1) They cease too early. So soon as the man really enters into his occupation his education ceases. (2) They are too narrow, they fail to provide experiences that give proper perspective; they do not give adequate theoretical comprehension of the work being accomplished from day to day; they do not develop the judgment.

The weakness with the Theoretical-practical method of providing experience resembles <p 266> the weakness of the Haphazard and the Apprenticeship methods in that it ceases too early. It ceases *before the individual begins his life work. It may have the special weakness of not being closely organized with the vocation for which it is assumed to be a preparation, hence of being impracticable.

The Practical-theoretical form of providing experience is based on two assumptions: The first assumption is that the practical and the theoretical should be equally emphasized; that they should be closely organized; and that the theory should be deduced from the practice. The second assumption is that the educative processes should continue so long as the man is engaged in his occupation.

A concrete illustration will make clear the difference between the four different methods of acquiring experience as given above.

During the present summer vacation I have been spending a few weeks in a boarding house. Some previous boarder had bequeathed to the house an intricate Chinese block puzzle. During this summer one lad in the house spent <p 267> eight hours in solving the puzzle. He worked by the Haphazard method, trying blindly, till he just happened to get it right. The next attempt did not take so long, but it was many days before he could solve the problem rapidly.

As soon as the lad had learned to solve the puzzle, my son watched him solve it many times, and kept trying to do it as he saw it done. My son learned to solve the puzzle in perhaps two hours by thus watching another and then trying it himself. He was employing the Apprenticeship method, and his education was accomplished in one fourth the time required by the Haphazard method.

In the boarding house was an expert mechanical engineer. He took up the task of solving the problem and was most scientific in his procedure. He figured out the principles that he thought might be involved, tried them, and immediately abandoned methods that proved unsuccessful. He was able to solve the puzzle in a half hour. Later trials were all successful and rapid. He knew just how he had solved the puzzle, and therefore <p 268> did not have to experiment or take chances on later trials. This engineer employed the Theoretical-practical method of learning.

The engineer volunteered to instruct me in the problem. I took up the blocks and began trying to unite them. As one difficulty after another arose, I was given instruction in the principle for overcoming it. No principle was presented to me till I had faced a situation demanding that particular principle. The practice and the theory went together, and so far as the instruction was concerned the practice preceded the theory step by step. I was therefore employing the Practical-theoretical method. As a result I was enabled to solve the problem in fifteen minutes. Furthermore I knew just how I had done it and could do it again and could apply the same principles to other puzzles.

A comparison of these results is most instructive. The lad who went at it blindly by the Haphazard method required eight hours and even then did not analyze out the principles that would help him solve later prob- <p 269> lems. My son, who employed the Apprenticeship method, accomplished his task in two hours but discovered no principles. His work was blindly mechanical. The engineer worked according to the Theoretical-practical method, completed his task in thirty minutes, and understood perfectly what he had done. By employing the Practical-theoretical method I was enabled to accomplish the task in fifteen minutes and to understand also how it was done.

Whether I have in mind my own development or that of my employees, if I am seeking to utilize the Practical-theoretical method of capitalizing experience, I am confronted with two problems: (1) How shall I secure or provide the requisite practical experiences? (2) How shall I secure or provide the appropriate theoretical interpretation of such experiences?

During recent years in the educational, industrial, and commercial world serious attempts have been made to answer these two questions, and the results are most significant.

The College of Engineering of the University of Cincinnati believes that it has solved the problem for certain fields of activity by ``co<o:>perative courses." In these courses the students spend one week in some manufacturing plant and the next week in the college. This weekly alternation of practical and theoretical is kept up for six years. The number of students in the college and the number of workers in the manufacturing plant is kept constant by dividing each group of students into two sections which alternate with each other, so that when one section is at the college the other is at the shop. The college teaches the principles that are necessary for understanding and solving the problems arising from week to week in the shop. As the Dean of the college expresses it, ``It aims to teach the theory underlying the work, to teach the intent of the work, to give such cultural subjects as will tend to make him a more intelligent civic unit."

www.ingramcontent.com/pod-product-compliance
Lightning Source LLC
Chambersburg PA
CBHW081818200326
41597CB00023B/4291